Facing And Surviving
PROSTATE CANCER
Today

The Book Patients Need To Read

J. Cheney Mason

&

Jeffrey Richard Thill, M.D.

Copyright © 2024 by J. Cheney Mason & Jeffrey Richard Thill, M.D.
All Rights Reserved

No part of this publication may be reproduced, stored in a retrieval system, or transmitted in any form or by any means, electronic, mechanical, photocopying, recording, scanning, or otherwise, without the prior written permission of the author.

An important note: This book is not intended as a substitute for the medical recommendation of physicians or other health-care providers. Rather, it is intended to offer information to help the reader cooperate with physicians and health professionals in a mutual quest for optimum well-being.

The identities of people described in the case histories have been changed to protect patient confidentiality.

The publisher and the author are not responsible for any goods and/or services offered or referred to in this book and expressly disclaim all liability in connection with the fulfillment of orders for any such goods and/or services and for any damage, loss, or expense to person or property arising out of or relating to them.

First edition 2024

ISBN: 978-1-917096-21-8

Written by a patient (non-doctor)

and a doctor (non-patient).

Contents

Introduction ix
1 Charley and The Diagnosis 1
2 The Biopsy 12
3 Learning and Deciding 21
4 The Harvard Medical School Annual Journal 30
5 PSA Testing and Recent Theories 38
6 Side Effects 45
7 Kegel Exercises 50
8 Gleason Scores 54
9 Learning The Options 60

10 The Robot 70
11 Bone Scan and A Decision 73
12 Preparing For Surgery 84
13 The Day Of Surgery 96
14 Going Home 109
15 Catheter 114
Conclusion 129
Glossary Of Supplies Needed Post-Surgery 133

Primary Sources of Information

Harvard Medical School Urology Department Annual

Journal on Prostate Diseases (2022)

American Cancer Society

American Urology Association

The Cleveland Clinic

National Comprehensive Cancer Network

Prostate Cancer Research Institute (PCRI)

Introduction

This book is essentially the history of the author's (Mason) actual process of discovery, treatment, and recovery of prostate cancer. Throughout, it is also discussions and information, without separate identity, by co-author Dr. Jeffrey Thill.

It has been approximately 20 years since I began my efforts to write this book about prostate cancer. I am not a medical doctor; I am now a mostly retired trial lawyer. I recently have also obtained a categorical title that I never wanted: widower. Initially, when I wanted to write this book, it was intended to be entitled "Prostate Cancer and Us". My thoughts were that I would outline the history of my own experiences and what I had learned and then follow different sections with revelations of impact, thoughts, and positions of my wife, Shirley. Until very recently, I had thought she had declined to write "her part" of the book; finding it to be too emotional and difficult. Even though we discussed it on numerous occasions, and she shared some thoughts with me, she just did not want to commit to writing—or so I thought!

As a result of Shirley's hesitancy, this project gradually got put more and more to the side. After a while, it just went into a folder and has remained there until now. Unfortunately, after all these years, I lost Shirley. We had been married for 48 years. I now feel the necessity of some form of "closure" (whatever that is) to finalize this book. Recently, and I presume by mere coincidence, I have had a repeated rash of confrontations with friends and friends of friends, asking me about what I knew about prostate cancer, them having learned that I had experienced it firsthand. Again, I hasten to remind all: I am not a doctor. However, from the beginning of my efforts to write this book, I have done so with consultation, as well as contributions from my life-saving surgeon (and co-author), Dr. Jeffrey Thill. Revealing the changes in our lives over the last 20 years, he has significantly changed his practice and semi-retired. On the other hand, I have continued to slog through the mud of life, both as a criminal and divorce lawyer, grandfather, now great-grandfather, and widower.

Having now recommitted to give my best efforts to finish this project, I started re-reading my original manuscript. It became clear that I needed to research and learn what new "science" or medical information there might be. Hoping that there might be revelations of major changes and potential therapies that might even benefit me, I dug in. Now, of course, the world is different in most regards. When I started the initial project, we did not have the advantage of the computer world and internet research that is now available. I quickly learned that the "go-to" source would be the esteemed Harvard Medical School, which publishes an Annual Report on prostate diseases. I obtained the 2022 Annual Report which is approximately 125 pages. Again, reiterating that I am not a doctor, I read all of it. What I came away with is the comfort of knowing that I had authoritative support for my understanding. I also gleaned that, apparently, there has been no real progress in treatment or prevention. The "disease" is omnipresent in men of numerous ages. It appears to me while there may be disagreement from more qualified people than I, virtually every male will experience and must endure prostate cancer if they live long enough. In fact, I found no indication of any changes from what I had learned years ago: every man will experience prostate cancer in various degrees unless he dies from something else before that.

I guess at some point, I needed to go ahead and get this project started. I have, of course, procrastinated, which is exactly how I find myself in this position to begin with. The purpose of doing this is not a commercial one, but rather one to try to help my friends with their future, and to that end, I will do my best to honestly reveal my inner thoughts, feelings, pains, discomforts, and as much detail as I have learned about the process. By doing that, some of you may avoid unnecessary unpleasantries and otherwise be better prepared than I initially was.

So that there can be no mistake, please remember that I am, for the umpteenth time, not claiming to be a doctor. You should consult with your own doctor to get answers (if possible) to all your questions. I respectfully suggest that you refer any questions that may be generated from this book to whoever he or she is and obtain your own copies of the Annual Report by Harvard Medical School on prostate cancer.

Having clarified the positions and explanations of my tardiness in finishing this book, I hope that you will be encouraged to help yourself and improve your education for the benefit of yourself and your family by reading how this project began, now 20 years ago.

Having committed to giving my best effort to finalize this book, I began reviewing my notes. By "twilight zone" intervention, my personal assistant and my housekeeper discovered a file that I had never seen before or even been aware of. My wife, having previously disclosed a reluctance to reveal her soul and write in this book, had, in fact, started a file. She handwrote numerous pages of notes and gathered together significant research. She had a degree in computer science, summa cum laude, from the most difficult computer science college in the country: University of Central Florida. All of her friends knew that she could, in essence, research anything and, as one good friend characterized her, she could "analyze the type off the page." Discovered in this mysteriously appearing file were, in essence, the following notes:

Wife's Surprise Revelations

I am on an airplane, traveling to one of my favorite destinations in the U.S... Santa Fe, New Mexico. The mystical, captivating Santa Fe. So, I am captive on an aircraft 35,000 feet in the air with not much to do but whatever I want that doesn't require movement. Well, I could read that book about the reconstruction of Paris that I haven't had time to devote to, or I could sit here and reflect on the last months of my life. Write them on paper and hope they help someone who is unfortunate enough to need my help. That was a rather long introduction and also a very telling one about how much I want to do this project. It's not that I don't want to share my knowledge and experience with those who need it; I want to give all that I can, but the difficulty in writing about my experience emanates from my inherent personal trait of being honest. Oh, you're probably thinking that's easy, just pen what you feel - no, it is not. You see, writing requires analyzation and an understanding of the subject. Oh, I learned that long ago in college. Write a paper and you will understand all you don't understand. This "paper" will make me come to terms with my deepest feelings about my experience with my husband's prostate cancer, and that is not an easy task. Oh God, can't I just have a research paper to do? Oh, well, here goes...

It all started seven months ago when we heard the diagnosis. Note I have changed to "we" because life is about "we" when couples nurture one another as we do especially in times of crisis.

Four months ago, my husband told me that he wanted to write about his experience with prostate cancer so that he might share his insight on a more personal, less medical level with those who were to come after him. No doubt, there will be way too many men, as the mantra now is "all men get prostate cancer if they live long enough". Well, I thought that was a great idea—a kind of man-to-man talk—an opening rep of the—soul—a revelation of one's inner self that helps someone else inch through a terrible time. "Great," I told him, that's really admirable. That is what women do all the time—we help our girlfriends get through. We talk, we reveal, we laugh, and we cry for one another. We are there for each other. However, when my darling announced that he wanted me to add my perspective to his creative work, I wasn't quite so enthusiastic. Not that I don't want to be the nurturer or that I can, but it's back to honesty. How do I come to terms with this ordeal and honestly write my thoughts and feelings on a piece of paper so that I might "get someone else through it"? Hell, I don't know that I want to know how I did it. I don't know that I want to come to terms with what I felt or what I feel now. But I guess I will because it may help "you" or your friend survive this time in your life when you need a friend who understands quite desperately. I remember so well the night of the fateful telephone call when we received the results of the biopsy. Oh, the weeks before leading up to the diagnosis were intense, but as a woman, I went on edge before every exam waiting for the results of "my mam or my pap"—and then had hope for enough to be pleasantly relieved by positive results. So, while the alert that the doctor felt some lumps in my husband's prostate was alarming, it was easy enough to put that into the back of my brain for later.

The biopsy procedure brought it all a bit closer to the reality of what might be, but it was not an end to the process.

So on we went with our daily routine. It was especially comforting hearing the doctor's words after the biopsy, "I don't think you should worry," so then we told the doctors we wanted the results via telephone. We could not wait for the appointment, which was weeks later.

Back to the night of the telephone call with the results. My husband answered the phone and I could see and felt by the look on his face what he had just been told. I watched his face melt. I don't know how to describe it any other way. I saw him shake his head—"Yes, I do have cancer."

So, where do we go from here? We don't know anything about prostate cancer. Hell, we are young; why should we know about this? My father died of cancer, my mother had lymphoma and is still alive—but those were my parents. We are too young and too ignorant about this disease. But now, I have to know—now we have to research—now I have to face mortality—oh, what a night

You know, relationships and marriages are interesting. If you are fortunate enough to survive the pitfalls and foibles of all that can go awry and finally come back to the emotional commitment that you started with, then I am a cheerleader for that. Oh yes, it's different than in the beginning. It's much better and the commitment deeper—but the vibrancy is there again, and the belief that nothing can go wrong is a myth.

But through the years, relationships take on a life of their own. What works for one couple is only known to them, and I think most of the time, you don't talk about why it works—it just does. But for all of us, what works and goes unsaid is that when one is weak, the other is strong. Well, of course, that's not something to discuss with a man. But that's the way it is. It is a silent thought that weaves itself through a small partnership. Well, who needs to be strong now? I am desperately trying–but everything is so unknown, and we didn't verbalize what we know our relationship held. And as always, no matter how close you are, some things just go unsaid, and you feel them.

So, yes, we were strong–each for the other, often we cried.

Those first nights of ignorance about the disease were horrible. I can only remember spending my days in a fog–thinking it could not possibly be true. My strong, overly-testosteroned husband had prostate cancer. I didn't know all the consequences, but I had some general knowledge, and it didn't make it feel any better. So, knowing I didn't know–made me want to know what I didn't know–to a certain degree.

How unusual for me not to want to know everything. I am the person who researches anything, any question that someone asks me that I don't know the answer to (yes, a bit obsessive–but that's not all bad). So what did I see happening? My husband's doctors were insistent that he educate himself on prostate cancer, and to that end, he was sent home with books to read so he would know all of his options and the consequences.

I focused my efforts on researching who and where provided the best treatment options–for every treatment that existed–I wanted to know who was the best. Maybe that was a good way to divide the research–but I knew in my heart that I could not bear to read about the treatments and the resulting impact. This was my husband, my overly macho, truth-charging husband, who I couldn't possibly imagine dealing with this diagnosis. I knew this would change our lives. I didn't know how, but I was frightened!

1

Charley and The Diagnosis

The story begins in early March of 2003 when, unexpectedly, I found myself with a couple of days of no calendar obligations, something that I do not remember seeing in years, except when I was on vacation. At any rate, my guardian angel somehow got through the thickness of my skull and suggested to me that now would be a perfect time to call my doctor and schedule my annual checkup. For years, I had faithfully gone for this yearly exam every one and a half to every two and half years! Well, this was no different, so I called my long-term physician and very dear friend and told him of my fortune with the time and asked if it was possible that he may be able to squeeze me in with my checkup. He, of course, was elated and quickly grabbed my file, admonished me that I was eight months late in following up with my check up, and said that he would see me the next morning at 8:30. Well, that felt pretty good; I would get this over with, this bother out of my way and score points with my wife for having done it. And away we go.

The next morning, I arrived at his office almost exactly on time, meaning that I was no more than two or three minutes late. Coming from across town with the early morning traffic made that somewhat of a miracle. Nevertheless, I got there and was greeted warmly by his staff, many of whom I have represented in one civil capacity or another. I have a good relationship with this doctor; not only are we friends, but I had been his personal lawyer for about 30 years and he'd been my doctor for the same time. He has also treated numerous friends of mine that I've referred to him over the years.

My wait to see the doctor was very minimal. I had barely started looking at an old boating magazine when I was called in for the initial routines, you know, the weight, the height, the two tubes of blood. Hell, they may have taken three; I don't know, I don't look, I can't stand to look. I never have been able to look at needles going in my arms. That is not natural. Nevertheless, having completed that and found that my blood pressure was only elevated just a little bit, obviously due to the 45 minutes in traffic attempting to get there on time, I was taken into another room. Here, they hooked me up and performed a routine EKG, which I was happy to hear revealed a normal heart tracing. Then, I was taken into an examining room to wait for Charley to finish up with his legitimate patients. Only a few minutes passed, and he came in, and I knew what was coming. I knew that he would go through the routine, you know, look in my eyes, look in my nose, look in my ears, look in my throat, listen to my chest, poke around my stomach, listen to my neck, do all those things that good doctors do, followed by the inevitable—the attack from the rear.

This, of course, was the big reason that I had procrastinated and not wanted to schedule this appointment. I dearly can't stand those needles by the girls in the front, but I would choose a needle any day over Mr. KY and a finger prodding my rectum—friend or not friend. In fact, maybe I would rather have a stranger—but dammit, I don't want to ever do it again. So, here it comes, Charley said, "Drop 'em and turn around." You know what that means, guys—put your elbows on the damn table, lean over, and wait for this guy to show you how super strong he is. With one finger, he could lift 200 pounds and move you around like a hot air balloon on a string. Well, once that injustice was over, I had to deal with that stuff running down my legs, simultaneously sticky and wet. My friend/client/doctor handed me the bag of chem wipes without a word so I could do my best in a very awkward situation to try to clean myself. No courtroom ever made me feel quite as vulnerable as this.

After getting myself together, I turned around to Charley, who had still not said a word. I noticed that the look on his face was not his normal jovial type of expression. The word 'consternation' seemed appropriate. "Well, Charley." I said, "What do you think?" He looked at me, and he paused just a moment. By that very pause, I knew that there was something about to be said that I was not going to like. Charley stood, looked at me, and said, "Cheney, I felt a couple of nodules on your prostate gland that I don't like, and I want you to see a urologist immediately." Wham! His statement caused an immediate rise in my temperature, undoubtedly my blood pressure, and certainly a feeling of being in a void and not knowing where I came from or where in the hell I was. But being the old bulletproof G.I. that I have been, and as they say—courtroom war horse—I figured that, well, this was something that would pass. Maybe it was a reaction to drinking too much wine, for which I could certainly be a fully guilty candidate. At any rate, we talked about going to a urologist. I had been to a urologist before—you know, that annual check that I do every three years. So, immediately, his staff made the appointment, and I told him I would go to my office and confirm the availability with my trial calendar and certainly give it a high priority. They did, and I did.

I remember leaving and calling my wife from my car. I knew Shirley was waiting to hear what Charley had to say, although we didn't have any great anxiety about anything because I seemed to be quite normally healthy and without any symptoms, complaints, or concerns from head to toe. So, I told her, "Well, you know, Charley said he felt something, and I've got to go to a urologist, and I'm getting that set up as soon as possible."

Well, I got back to my office, checked my calendar, and realized that my mind was starting to kind of fly away and not really concentrate or pay attention to anything on my desk or otherwise. Nevertheless, the appointment was made, and

I finished the day and went home. Shirley and I talked about it a little bit, but at this point, we had no great concern. For now, the only thing to do was wait.

One week later, I presented myself to the urologist. There we go again with blood tests, urine tests, the damn KY torpedo, and the awkward cleanup process. This time, the process was with a stranger doctor, a very nice fellow, but it didn't make any difference; you know, I thought maybe a stranger versus a friend—hell no. By the way, he's heard all the same jokes, you know, the ones like, "Make sure that urologist does not have both hands on your shoulders"—those types of things. I guess they're not even funny anymore. Probably weren't funny the first time I heard them other than it being the first time. I'm sure they'll be around forever, and I'm sure there's more I don't know and frankly don't care to learn at this point.

The doctor looked at me and said, "I agree with Dr. Williams. I did find and do feel some nodules on the left side of your prostate gland, and you're going to have to have biopsies." Biopsies. The B word. Biopsies. Okay, I lost my breath, and then I asked, "When are we going to schedule them?" He replied that it should be as soon as possible, with only enough delay time to clear my system of supplements and things that may cause bleeding.

There was no running from it now. I was going to have to have it done. The sooner, the better; after all, I have had several friends in my life who had paved the way before me with prostate cancer and radical surgery. I didn't want that to happen if I could avoid it, so I wanted to get to it. They scheduled it, and I went back to my office and checked my calendar to move things around and confirm the appointment for the biopsies.

Of course, the trial that I had interrupted out of town in order to get with these processes was starting to meet with some objections from the wonderful, warm, lovely, and fuzzy lawyers from New York City representing an absolute liar husband. They wanted to take advantage of my rapidly increasing instability and concerns. The judge, however, was human. In fact, he wondered how I could even be over there at all anticipating the biopsies. Thus, while the lawyers from New York City wanted to move ahead and have more evidence of this drawn-out trial on the very day I was supposed to have biopsies, the judge sided with me. My medical situation being unknown was certainly more important than just listening to another day of lying testimony.

I stopped taking my Silver Centrum multi-vitamins, my vitamin E, and my Omega 3 flax seed oil pills that also include vitamin E (all of which can contribute to bleeding) and began the ten-day wait. I must tell you that only a liar would not admit that waiting and anticipating having biopsies to see whether you have prostate cancer is unnerving. It preoccupied my thoughts. It interfered with my concentration. I had already reached a certain level of "don't give a damn" about practicing. Of course, who wouldn't after 35 years (at that time) of being a trial lawyer? Nevertheless, I knew there were things that I had to do, and

I started wanting to just change things, cancel things, reschedule things, get all of these matters out of my way, off of my mind, and relieve my mental responsibilities so I could deal with this medical issue. That's what I began to do.

Within a couple of days, I received an information sheet that explained generally how the biopsy would be done and what I needed to do to prepare. I had never had any form of biopsy before, and I had many questions. Cutting a piece of something and examining it doesn't sound so bad until you start thinking about it. Doctors say it is no big deal, that you will go in and be able to leave quickly. But how the hell do they cut something out of your prostate gland that's in the middle of your abdomen? Do they stick something in your penis, up your urethra, to the prostate? No, that is completely wrong. A quick study of anatomy shows that the urethra goes straight up into the bladder, and the prostate is around it. What they must do is go through your rectum. They use an ultrasound, a tube that is maybe six or eight inches in length and probably about as big around as my thumb. Mounted to this, and part of this instrument is a carrier for needles. "Now, how does this work?" I wondered. The needle must go through the wall of the rectum, into the prostate gland, and be able to extract a piece. "Wait a minute," I thought, "this is not such a casual 'just drop by' deal after all!" The doctors may do it all the time, but of course, not to themselves.

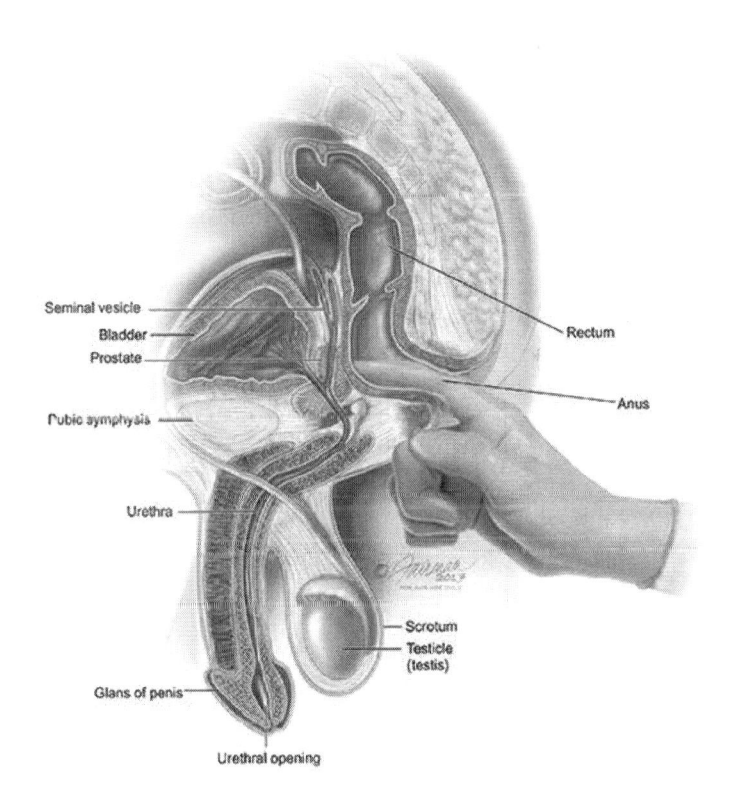

2

The Biopsy

The details of the biopsy began the day before the scheduled appointment. One day before arriving at the doctor's office, I was directed to take an antibiotic that would fight against potential infection from the outrageous procedure I was soon to undergo. For me, it was 500 mg of Cipro. I was also to become good friends with Mr. Fleets and his enema product. The Fleets would completely empty out my bowel. I was to have nothing but liquid until midnight and then a complete fast the day of the procedure. In many cases now, the patient is given medications other than IV sedation and is not required to fast.

On the morning of the biopsy, I went to the doctor's office, and the first thing to be done was, of course, to fill out another one of the damn forms–the same one I had already done a couple of times. They also did a urine test to make sure I didn't have any new infections. Next, a physician's assistant or nurse placed an IV in the back of my hand so that they could administer the drugs to basically knock me out. In my case, I was given a small dose of Versed plus a tiny dose of Fentanyl. Versed is a drug that has been used for years, originally back during the Cold War days with the CIA, to cause people to tell the truth or to go through something and not have any recollection of it. Some 90-plus percent of people who are administered Versed have no idea what happened during that period. For the past many years, patients have been given a Valium tablet only or a Valium tablet plus a pain pill. This is usually enough to relax the patient enough to insert the probe into the rectum.

A prostate local anesthetic block is then performed before any biopsies are taken.

The Versed took effect, and though I remember my procedure, there was nothing painful about it. I was helped to lay on my side on a table in the operating room while the attendants hooked up this, that, and the other equipment. Once the sonogram wand is inserted into a patient's rectum, the doctor can see what he is doing on the sonogram screen. It allows the doctor to accurately position the biopsy equipment so that he can shoot the needles through the rectum and into the suspicious areas of the prostate.

The needle is a piece of equipment that separates. It pulls itself apart lengthwise, shoots through the wall of the rectum, into the prostate gland, and springs back shut. As it springs shut, it cuts and traps a piece of the gland into the needle. Then, that one is withdrawn, and another goes in. In my situation, the doctor had determined from his exam that they would do twelve of these biopsies. That's twelve different times a needle was shot in, snapped, and bit to come out with a piece. That sounds a whole lot worse than it really is because it is very, very small. The feeling a patient has during a biopsy has been described as if someone had popped a rubber band against the back of their hand. That is a fair description of what I felt. I was conscious throughout this process, or at least I thought I was. I could hear, and I could feel the somewhat dull "pop, pop, pop" of these shots going into my gland. I heard all ten of them—but there were twelve.

After the twelve samples had been taken, the wand was withdrawn with no pain. I was not really aware of what was going on; I was just off the table, rested a little bit, and then taken back into kind of a holding area to sit and wait. I'm not sure what we were waiting for, I guess to make certain that nothing had gone wrong, which it hadn't. Then, I guess, prompted by the creation of the pressure from the biopsies, I really needed to urinate. I went into a little bathroom that was nearby. No one had prepared me for what would happen when I began to urinate. There was a whole lot of blood, or at least a lot of blood, for a person who's not used to doing it every day. Blood and blood clots. The stream of urine was more red than yellow, and it was somewhat scary.

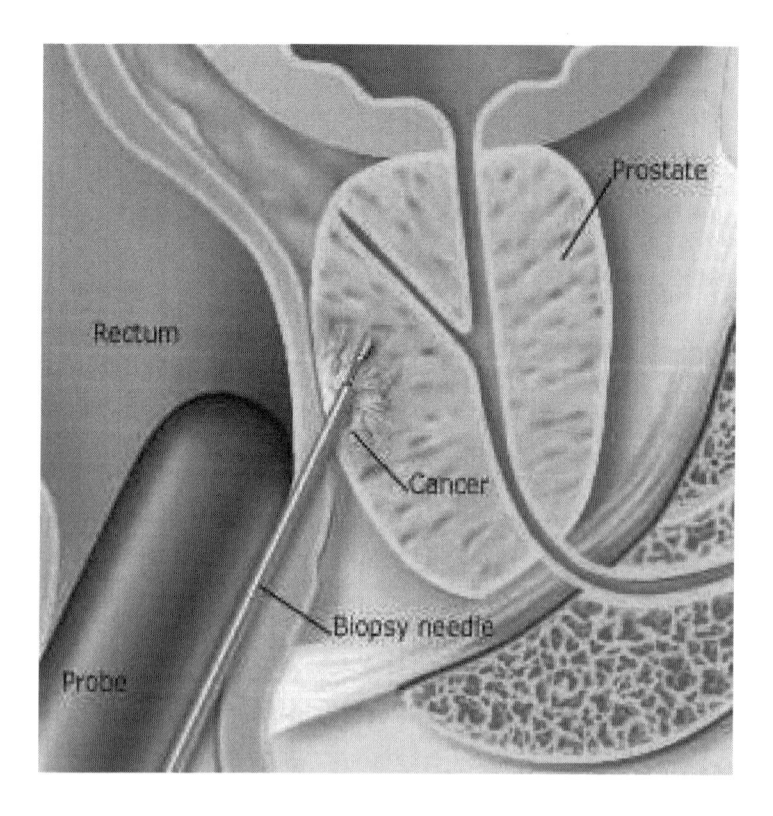

After that little shock, I was able to finish getting dressed and go home. The blood clots would continue over the next several days. They became less frequent and fewer, smaller and smaller, until there were just small flecks and the slight appearance of blood in my urine. This went on for several days, though I'm sure it varies with each person.

That's the biopsy process except for the following days of the bleeding and spotting in your underwear. I'm certain this causes no impression or evokes any sympathy from your wife or any other woman around, but it is somewhat concerning, at least on a small scale, to have blood spots in your underwear from your rectum. Patients may have a small amount of blood with their first bowel movement. The first time a patient ejaculates, there is A LOT of blood in the semen, and this can persist but diminishes over many weeks. For several days after the biopsy, it is recommended to eat a bland diet. You know, no good Mexican food or spicy Italian because you don't want to irritate your bowels. You also continue with the Cipro antibiotic process for the days of its prescription, which it seems to me was a total of about five, just to make sure that you don't have an infection because of the nature of the process itself.

You may experience discomfort following the biopsy; however, usually taking Tylenol should alleviate these symptoms. You should not take Aspirin or blood-thinning medications until the bleeding has stopped in your urine and stool unless otherwise specifically directed by your doctor. You should not engage in any strenuous activity for at least 24 hours. This would include ordinary things such as jogging, tennis, golf, bicycling, racquetball, heavy lifting, or even lawn mowing. You also should abstain from sexual activity for at least 24 hours. If you continue to have severe pain that is not relieved by Tylenol, or continue to have blood passing in your urine or stool for more than three days, or running a fever of one hundred degrees or more, you should contact your doctor.

While recovering from the biopsy, I also had to deal with my mind. I had now gone through the weeks of the first diagnosis, suspicion by my doctor/friend, waiting, confirmation by the specialist, waiting, the biopsies, and now waiting again for the biopsy results. The results are not something that is instantly rendered. The samples that were trapped in the separating needles that snapped and cut had to be given to the pathologist, where they were microscopically examined to determine whether or not they appeared to be cancerous and, if so, the degree and aggressive nature of the cancer.

During the waiting process, it felt as if all of my close friends and people around me were looking at me, wanting to ask me how it went and what the results were. Every time it came up, I started worrying more. There were only two answers. Either I had cancer, or I did not have cancer. There was no middle ground. At the time, the only thing I could say was, "I'm waiting; I haven't heard yet, I don't know." I was scheduled to start picking the jury in a first-degree murder case on the very day that the doctor had scheduled an appointment for me to come in for a consult, kind of like the old days of Marcus Welby, so he could tell me the news. Hell, I didn't want to wait for that, and I told this doctor to please not treat me like an ordinary patient. I felt I was a tough enough guy to hear the news, but I had so many complications in my life and my profession that I didn't have the luxury of just hanging around and waiting. I needed to know.

So I asked the doctor to please, when he got the results, just call me and tell me because it would change not just my life schedule or what I had to do or not do, but it would also affect dozens of other people and courts as to whether I could be there or couldn't be there. I knew I was not going to be able to go into a courtroom and try a case, or be competent otherwise, for anybody until I knew the results and then, of course, depending on what those results were–what kind of action I was going to have to take or not take.

3

Learning and Deciding

As revealed in my wife's recollection, we waited five days before we got the report from the doctor. He did call me at home in the evening as he had promised and as I had requested. As you can imagine, we were quite nervous. My wife and I were having dinner when the phone rang. As I picked it up and said, "Hello, Dr. Brady," I looked at my wife and saw an immediate frozen look on her face. We both, I guess, were privately concerned and anticipated it undoubtedly was going to be prostate cancer–after all, I was 61 years old, and it's just the kind of thing that happens, isn't it? Dr. Brady said, "Mr. Mason, you asked me to call, so I am." I knew before he said anything else because he hadn't given that prologue to what he was going to say; he would have said, "You're okay," but he didn't. He said, "The truth is, I have to tell you, you do have cancer. You know, we took twelve biopsies, six of those were positive for cancer. Some of it is more aggressive than the others, so we need to get you in to talk to me as soon as possible."

"Okay," I said, taking a breath and exhaling. What else the hell am I gonna do or say? I looked at my wife, and she saw clearly the look on my face and knew what exactly was being told to me on the phone. The doctor advised that there was a seminar to be held at his practice office the following evening for newly diagnosed patients and that he really wanted me to go to it so I'd learn more about what was going on before we met.

I thanked the doctor for the call, and I sat down and looked at my wife, and I had to just tell her–"Shirley, I've got cancer." Tears began in both of our eyes, but there was nothing else that could be said. We then agreed that we would do what had to be done. There are lots of ways to treat it, and we would find out just what my options were. We didn't know, but we would find out, discover the facts, and make decisions.

The next day, I was somewhat foggy-headed in going to work and wasn't particularly interested in doing anything so I asked my secretary to clear my calendar and cancel my appointments. When I felt up to it, about an hour or so later, I went down the hall to tell my two long-time partners that, in fact, the biopsies were not good and that I did have cancer. Of course, they were deflated instantly and concerned. None of us had any idea what would happen next. We talked about what it would mean and that we would have to wait and see just exactly the extent and the treatment, but that the options were different forms of radiation treatment, perhaps chemotherapy, and surgery.

At this point, I was really losing the ability to focus on what I was supposed to be doing or not doing. My secretary went into somewhat of a panic when I told her the news and asked her to cancel the appointments. I told her there was nothing we could do about it like that, just take care of the business and we'll do what we can. I returned a few phone calls and hung around for a while but realized I wasn't accomplishing a damn thing. My mind was entirely elsewhere. I wondered what I was going to do, how I should do it, and the impact. I wondered if I was going to die from this because prostate cancer is purportedly the second leading killer of men in our society after lung disease. I called a very good friend of mine, a top flight medical malpractice/personal injury lawyer out of town who I had handled cases with over the years. I got him on the phone and told him about the diagnosis. His reaction was as predictable as any friend's would be—"O my God." He then promptly iterated, "Well, you know what, it's not something you're gonna die from." He went on to tell me that he had been involved in the handling of various malpractice cases involving prostate surgery over the years, and he'd gotten pretty well-schooled in it. He had a friend, a doctor, who was the head of the urology department at Shands Teaching Hospital in Gainesville, and he would ensure that I had an appointment with him personally for a consult as soon as possible.

At this same time, I was feeling simultaneously somewhat obligated to share my diagnosis with my friends and also afraid of talking about it. I was not embarrassed; it had never really entered my mind to say I was embarrassed about it. I was concerned about what to do. Probably the closest friend in my life that I've had for a long, long, long time, measured in a handful of decades, unfortunately, went through this same process himself six years earlier. He kept it a complete secret until it was over, which I found to be somewhat offensive, and I told him so. He had complete open surgery where they had to split him from the pubic bone to the naval to remove the prostate gland. When I told Bill that I had biopsies and a diagnosis of cancer, he told me that the hardest thing that he had to do after his diagnosis was tell his children. We both have two daughters, and I understood that. I had not told either of my daughters that I was suspected of having prostate cancer because, of course, I'd hoped that the biopsies would somehow be negative, and therefore, telling them would have created unnecessary anxiety for them. Of course, I knew that by calling them and telling them now, they would be angry at Dad for not telling them before, but I had to make a choice between the evils, and that's what it was. Only my wife and her mother, the two friends that I had talked to, and the fellows at the office knew that I was even under suspicion and had gone through the biopsy process.

Now, I had to start telling clients whose cases I was putting on hold and judges whose schedules I was not going to keep the circumstances of my condition. Boy, this was just a great deal of fun. The only thing I can say for sure is that all of them were immediately completely understanding and sympathetic and did what could be done to accommodate me in every way possible. Starting that process and getting out of work, closing cases out, delaying them, and talking to other lawyers and judges as necessary consumed the next couple of days.

The next stop was the seminar to find out our options and as much as possible about this process. Before going to the seminar, I was invited to stop by the doctor's office that afternoon and pick up a package of videotapes, books, and pamphlets on the "So You Have Prostate Cancer" type mode. I didn't know whether I wanted to read them or throw them away, but I decided I didn't have much choice. I needed to find out everything that I could, and of course, my wife was on that project with me. She was analytical about everything. There was no way in the world we were not going to do it in that fashion. I went by and picked up the books, came home, had a glass of wine, talked about it, and began reading.

I must say that there is no question of the value of reading and understanding as much as you possibly can about this damn disease. We don't grow up knowing about it. We grow up with myths, misinformation, errors, and fantasies. We don't really know where the prostate is, what it does, what it doesn't do, and how important or unimportant it is to us. The only thing we know for sure growing up is that cancer is bad, is bad, is bad, is bad. There ain't no good cancer! Maybe that's not exactly true. I guess if you're a man, you're gonna have some cancer unless it's something on your arm or your ear, and it can just be lanced off and be done; there's no question in my mind that you want to stand in the prostate line and hope that you get called for it as opposed to something else because the truth of the matter is that prostate cancer is very treatable. It's just a hell of a process to go through.

So I started looking in the books, reading all about it, and learning at age 61 what's really inside my body—at least part of it—that I was not fully aware of before, and understanding how everything works and how it's all tied together. The information started to alert us to such things as how diet can impact prostate cancer and how it can actually slow the process in many circumstances. It was greatly interesting to learn about such beneficial things as green tea and lycopene from stewed tomatoes. You know, eat your pasta and your pizza.

Well at any rate, we were now in the process of, okay, educate, consult, learn what to do. All I knew for a fact was that I had six out of twelve biopsies positive for prostate cancer, some worse areas than others, and I had to find out what that meant.

4

The Harvard Medical School Annual Journal

Your current primary physician or urologist may or may not have available in their office any reading materials that are up-to-date and meaningful to a discussion of your diagnosis. The Harvard Medical School presents a detailed annual report on prostate diseases. While it may be more detailed and lengthy than most people would want, I certainly recommend that you at least discuss it with your doctor. If he or she is not particularly up to date, then I would do two things: get a new doctor and seek a copy of the annual journal from Harvard.

Most recently, there has been regulatory approval of two imaging agents that reveal new metastatic prostate tumors. This is done by injecting certain compounds that travel in the bloodstream until they encounter what is known as "prostate-specific membrane antigen." This, according to the journal, is allowing doctors to treat tumors that might otherwise have been missed. I view this as a dramatic statement and is born out, indeed, by the board of Harvard doctors that specialize in this. There are, in addition, important advances regarding genetic testing that can reveal an increased risk of developing prostate cancer. They are also investigating hormonal therapy for treatment. According to the journal, hormonal treatment has complexities that might not otherwise be anticipated. Standard hormonal therapies block testosterone. Further, according to the journal, this form of treatment reduces pain and generally delays tumor progression. However, there are side effects, including nausea, liver problems, fatigue, metabolic syndrome, and an acceleration of coronary artery disease. Still being questioned is also the apparent increase in the risk of falling. They do not know or claim why this occurs, but apparently, the treatment may decrease skeletal muscle mass and strength.

There have been some claims that some treatments may impact cognitive processes that have previously been known as "chemo fog" or brain fog, resulting in erectile dysfunction. However, according to the journal, they have no conclusive findings in that regard. With hormone therapy, brain fog is an issue.

Current medical thinking concurs with prior beliefs that black men inherit approximately twice the risk of prostate cancer, on average, than white men. It also appears that Asians have the lowest genetic risk of prostate cancer.

Another important recognition is that despite many people having concerns or worry about erectile function following prostate biopsies, that appears not to be accurate.

According to the journal, while some effects on erectile function are recognized in the first few weeks after a biopsy, most men regain sexual potency within a few months. Only repeated biopsies, three or more, are associated with erectile dysfunction.

Somewhat alarming is that contrary to the general belief that COVID-19 was generally thought to affect only lungs and upper airways, recent researchers have found that the virus may exacerbate benign prostate symptoms.

Apparently, there are some other issues that should be addressed and recognized. Some men apparently worry that prostatitis is contagious. According to the annual journal from Harvard, that simply is not true. Further, there is no proof of a direct connection between prostatitis and prostate cancer.

Prostate cancer is the second most commonly diagnosed cancer in men in the United States and the second leading cause of cancer death among men (after lung cancer). Generally, men are diagnosed with prostate cancer after blood tests reveal abnormal levels of prostate specific antigen (PSA). While there does not, as of today, exist knowledge of precise causes of prostate cancer, this is also apparently a disease that is inherited or may be inherited genetically.

Some of the known sources or risk factors are issues that should be discussed specifically with your doctors. They include but are not necessarily limited to the following:

Age: About 90% of prostate cancer diseases are diagnosed in men over age 55, and the median age for diagnosis is 66. Prostate cancer runs in families.

Race: As I stated above, in the United States, black men have the highest prostate cancer incidents and death rates of any group. Prostate cancer incidents vary greatly among countries. The highest rates are in Australia, New Zealand, Western Europe, Canada, United States, and the Caribbean, while the lowest rates are in South Central Asia and Northern Africa.

Obesity: Increases the risk of developing and dying from aggressive prostate cancer. This is particularly true with men who are overweight during their 50s and 60s.

Diet: Another factor to be considered; men who eat a lot of red meat or high-fat dairy products seem to have a higher risk. Diets high in cholesterol and saturated fat, usually found in fatty beef and cheese, are a recognized problem. Diets that are rich in fruit and vegetables may reduce the risk of prostate cancer. One frequently discussed impact of vegetables is related to lycopene, the compound that gives tomatoes their bright red hue. Some research has shown that two servings of tomato sauce a week seem to be enough to give some protection.

People who consume a Mediterranean diet appear to have much lower prostate cancer death rates. Additionally, studies have found that men who eat moderate to high amounts of fish are less likely to develop prostate cancer or die from it compared to men who do not.

Dietary supplements should also be considered. Vitamin E supplementation has been shown to increase the rate of prostate cancer developed when it was tested in certain circumstances. At the same time, the consumption of very low levels of Vitamin D has been shown to increase the risk of advanced prostate tumors. It is also believed, therefore, that increasing intake of Vitamin D might be one potential way to reduce overall risk. Statins frequently used to deal with reducing cholesterol might lower the risk of prostate cancer.

Alcohol use has resulted in conflicting results. Apparently, drinking moderate amounts of red wine increases the risk of prostate cancer, yet moderate white wine consumption may have a protective effect. In general, however, apparently, alcohol used in moderation poses little to no risk of prostate cancer. I guess the concern here is the definition of "moderate".

Physical and sexual activity can also affect risk. The Harvard studies reveal that men who engaged in the most frequent and vigorous activity had a 30% lower risk of developing advanced prostate cancer and a 25% lower risk of dying from it.

Similarly, researchers found men who ejaculate frequently have a lower risk of prostate cancer. One of the studies reveals that men who ejaculate more than twenty-one times per month had a 20% lower prostate cancer risk than those who ejaculate four to seven times a month.

Another occasionally discussed concern is whether or not vasectomies will increase the risk of prostate cancer. At this point, there is no firm conclusion that cancer risk to the prostate is increased as a result of vasectomies.

While the above risk factors are important to consider, it is most important for people to recognize that most men with prostate cancer do not have any symptoms in the initial stages of the disease. For this reason, regular checkups at your doctor's office are critical.

5

PSA Testing and Recent Theories

From time to time, I have observed stories printed in various national newspapers that discuss prostate tests. Without detailed explanation, many of these stories have simply made bold statements that men should not take the PSA tests and/or that doing so was dangerous. My continued reasoning and research simply is that those statements are ridiculous. A PSA test is only a blood test. We routinely have blood tests for numerous issues, and other than the tiny needle prick in the arm vein, there is nothing to be concerned about. It is simply a matter of diagnosis. PSA trends may be more important than a single PSA result, especially PSA readings doubling in a short time. For example, comparing the histories of two patients, both aged 62, is revealing. Patient #1 had PSA tests yearly, resulting in readings of 3.0, 2.9, 3.1, 3.2, and 3.3. Patient #2 had readings of 0.9, 0.9, 1.0, 1.1, and then 3.3. This comparison reveals that patient #1's readings were basically the same for the period of time, whereas patient #2 had his PSAs triple in a year and is, therefore, in trouble. In an effort to try to provide general information about what to do with anything regarding prostate cancer, there are general characterizations. Prostate cancer can be considered low risk and low volume, low risk and high volume, intermediate risk with low or high volume, and high risk with low or high volume. If a diagnosis is generally low risk and low volume, that is a candidate for active surveillance.

The PSA tests have been recommended for decades. At different times, different medical organizations changed the recommended age at which PSA tests should be administered. There are numerous interpretations of what a PSA test scoring may mean and what if any, additional inquiries should be made. It appears to me, based on all of my years of research, that a PSA test is not only safe but very important. However, it must be remembered that it is only a test, and there are others, in addition to that, that would be considered by a competent urologist. Normally, a PSA test with certain readings will prompt the physician to further seek and perform a DRE (Digital Rectal Exam). These two tests may reveal an additional suggestion that biopsies be taken, which will thus confirm or deny suspected cancerous tumors in the prostate. This issue is something that should be discussed with your urologist with specificity and in detail.

There is now, fairly recently (since 2012), what is known as a Prostate Health Index (PHI). This new testing evaluation appears to be accepted by the overall expert medical community as significant in trying to determine the presence or absence of prostate cancer and, therefore, treatment thereof.

As research continues, there has now been developed a process of being able to reasonably pinpoint prostate cancerous tumors that have metastasized, even after surgery. There appears to be very encouraging scientific research allowing pinpointing of cases where a man's PSA levels were rising after surgery. This process and the research are current and active. It should be discussed with specificity with your doctor, who, hopefully, is kept abreast of the developments and research as revealed by the Harvard Medical School and the Food and Drug Administration.

One of the most frequently discussed considerations regarding potential prostate problems is whether there should be intervention by surgery or take a "wait and see" position by continued surveillance. I have known many fellows who took the "wait and see" who then had to have surgery, some who died, and others who are still under surveillance years after beginning it. According to the research that I have done, it appears that there is no universally agreed-upon process for deciding which approach to take. The decision as to whether to follow surveillance, further testing, or surgery is a complex one. As there has been an increase in awareness and revelation of the entire subject matter over the past few years, it has become more complex. There appear to be a number of medications that have been approved for various anticipated treatments. This subject should also be specifically discussed with your doctor before making any decision. Even then, you may find future reasons to change your decision as symptoms may occur, study and research may enhance positions, and new developments in the medical/surgical/scientific world are made.

As stated, the subject matter of prostate cancer and treatment continues to evolve with more and more theories and methods of treatment. While there is still no absolute cure or prevention, there are different studies being reported that reveal combinations of treatments with promising indications. It has been reported by the National Cancer Institute that men with metastatic prostate cancer lived longer if they started chemotherapy along with hormonal therapy instead of going on hormonal therapy by itself. Currently, there are studies utilizing the concept of attempting to cut off the blood supply to the individual suspected tumors. This revealing evolution has been provided by my grandson, Mason Gardner, currently a medical student at the University of Mississippi Medical Center. Back in April of 2004, several men with prostate cancer showed up at Canadian hospitals for one-time injections of experimental drugs designed to eradicate the tumors. Radiation had already failed. After about ten months, the tumors had shrunk by as much as 84%. The experimental drug used worked its way through the bloodstream but became toxic only when exposed to light.

Doctors focus laser light onto the skin or internal tumor using catheter-inserted optical fibers. The drugs killed just the illuminated issue and left unexposed tissue relatively unchanged. Photosynthesizes had been used for a decade against esophageal, bladder, lung, and skin cancers. Many doctors determined at that time that this was a very promising treatment for recurrent prostate cancers after radiation. Amongst the experts involved with that, many concluded that if they had a choice between an experimental drug and the light treatment, they would choose it clearly over any surgery or radiation. Thus, experimentation in attacking cancerous tumors has been actively going on for a very long time and these studies and results now approximately twenty years ago give hope. One can only encourage increases in theories and attempts to both detect and potentially eradicate cancers without the necessity of a full radical prostatectomy.

6

Side Effects

Chemotherapy is frequently suggested and used, along with different medications. A concern that seems to be generally reported is the number of side effects that result. There is more than just predictable hair loss. A patient considering treatment options should further discuss with the doctor the various reported and, therefore, fairly predictable side effects. According to historical research, apparently, when prostate cancer metastasizes, it goes into the bones about 90% of the time. This has a dramatic increase in the likelihood of death. Additionally, the cancer can spread to other organs to a limited degree. According to the Harvard Annual Report, as recently as a decade ago, when prostate cancer metastasized into lymph nodes or bones, it was considered universally fatal and subject to very limited treatment. Active and intense evaluations and discussions among the professionals are constantly ongoing.

For many years, in fact, decades, most people refused to discuss issues related to prostate diseases. Just as television advertising would not even include the word "brassiere", much less any images, the words "erectile dysfunction" were completely taboo. Now, there does not seem to be any human personal issues that are not publicly discussed. Advertisements and discussions about "ED" (Erectile Dysfunction) are publicized almost hourly!

Surgical techniques attempting to do nerve-sparing are major and serious considerations. The process is not absolute or precise. However, substantial progress in avoiding ED has been reported. Despite continuous awareness and concerns about doing the "nerve-sparing surgery," it appears that only 10-20 % of men under sixty years of age regain the sexual potency that they had before surgery. The reported impact from surgery varies dramatically, with a low of 14% to a high of 90% having ED following surgery.

The surgery removes not just the prostate gland but also the seminal vesicles. Erectile dysfunction post-op is determined by surgeon experience, and whether neither, one, or both neurovascular bundles were spared. This eliminates the ability to ejaculate. Also, some men, for a period of time (approximately a year), would find any orgasm to be painful. This entire subject matter is "no pun intended or related" embryonic. As a reference to public disclosures and advertising, the subject matter of "ED" continues to be investigated

An additional major issue dealing with the entire subject matter is urinary incontinence. This is generally the most dreaded and unwelcome of all potential side effects from cancer treatment, even more so than erectile dysfunction. Doctors still cannot preoperatively determine which patients will have incontinence. Women are more prone to incontinence than men because women have only two urinary control mechanisms (bladder neck and the external sphincter). Men have three! (Bladder neck, external sphincter, and the prostate.) The external sphincter can also be thought of as the pelvic floor. Men rarely have to use their pelvic floor for urinary control. When the prostate is surgically removed, the pelvic floor has to step up! The bladder neck sphincter is physically separated from the prostate at the time of surgery, and the male urethra is cut just in front of the prostate, very close to the external sphincter/pelvic floor. The resulting "hole" at the bottom of the bladder has to be sewn to the urethral stump at the pelvic floor. Surgically, doctors try to preserve the bladder neck fibers and preserve as much urethra between the prostate and the external sphincter as possible. Prior to surgery, it is recommended that men do pelvic floor exercises, i.e., Kegel maneuvers.

7

Kegel Exercises

The Kegel exercises were developed in the late 1940s by Dr. Arnold H. Kegel, an American Gynecologist, as a non-surgical way to prevent women from leaking urine. They also work for men plagued by incontinence. Kegel exercise strengthens the pelvic floor muscle group, which is involved in stemming the flow of urine. By building up these muscles prior to surgery, you will speed up your return to continence afterward. Additionally, strengthening the pelvic floor muscles improves orgasmic function, and this will help you preserve and regain potency. In the interest of continence and potency, it is essential that you begin a consistent regimen as soon as possible and continue to maintain it faithfully after surgery.

To find the muscle, imagine you are at a party, and the rich food you have just consumed causes you to have gas. The muscle that you use to hold back gas is the one you want to exercise. Some people find this muscle by voluntarily stopping the stream of urine. Another way to find the muscle is by pulling your rectum and urethra up inside.

Begin by emptying your bladder. Then try to relax completely. Tighten this muscle and hold for a count of ten seconds, then relax the muscle completely for a count of ten seconds. You should feel a sensation of lifting the area around your urethra or of pulling around your rectum.

Exercise in the morning, the afternoon, and at night. Initially, you may not be able to hold the contraction for the complete count of ten. However, you will slowly build to ten-second contractions over time. The muscles may start to tire after six or eight exercises. If this happens, stop and go back to exercise later. These exercises can be practiced anywhere at any time. Most people seem to prefer exercising, lying on their bed, or sitting in a chair.

Never use your stomach, legs, or buttocks muscles. To find out if you are also contracting your stomach muscle, place your hand on your abdomen while you squeeze your pelvic muscle. If you feel your abdomen move, then you are also using these muscles. In time, you will learn to practice effortlessly. Eventually, work these exercises in as part of your lifestyle; tighten the muscles when you walk, before you sneeze, on the way to the bathroom, and when you stand up.

These exercises cannot harm you in any way. Most patients find them relaxing and easy. If you get back or stomach pain after you exercise, then you are probably trying too hard and using your stomach and back muscles.

On the entire subject matter, issues that should be discussed between the patient and the surgeon include but are not limited to, significant issues such as diet, exercise, weight, and alcohol. Interestingly, smoking can be a substantial issue. Apparently, smokers have a 24% higher risk of death from prostate cancer than non-smokers.

8

Gleason Scores

A uniform method of evaluating prostate cancers was developed by Doctor Gleason. This system has become the standard by which pathologists and lab personnel grade cancerous cells taken during biopsies. Basically, each of the tissue samples removed by a biopsy needle is studied by a pathologist and assigned a number grade from 1 to 5 based on how closely it resembles normal prostate tissue. A grade of 1 is normal, and a grade of 5 is very abnormal. When cancer is found, it is most often given a grade of three, four, or five. From the ten to twelve needle biopsies, a tumor may be found to have cancerous cells with different grades. Because of this, the two most common grades are then added together to come up with the Gleason Score. For example, if most of the tumor is grade 3 and less is grade 4, that patient's Gleason Score is 7 (3+4=7). If most of the tumor is grade 4 and less is grade 3, the Gleason Score will also be 7. This example, however, (4+3=7) indicates a more aggressive cancer than the 3+4=7. The higher the Gleason Score, the more aggressive the cancer is. A Gleason Score of 6 indicates a slow-growing cancer that is highly treatable. If the score is 8 or more, there is a high probability that the cancer cells will grow and metastasize. This is when prostate cancer becomes extremely dangerous. If the cancer spreads outside the prostate gland, it can go to the nearest lymph node chain in the pelvis or into the lumbar spine, hip, and ribs. Once cancer gets into the bones, it is very difficult to treat.

With the knowledge of a patient's Gleason Score, their age and lifestyle, the doctor and the patient will consider how aggressively they want to treat the cancer. A patient with a Gleason Score of 6 has a slow-growing cancer and may choose to modify their diet and take the "wait and see" approach. Many fellows that I know who had a Gleason Score of 7 have opted for the implantation of radiation seeds or radioactive seeds and/or otherwise received radiation treatment. I know some guys who have done the seeds and have claimed to be happy with the results and success after a couple of years. I know many others, however, who have found the experiment to have wholly failed. There can be issues with the implantation of radiation seeds. In this process, 40-80 radioactive seeds are injected into the prostate gland. They usually stay in the prostate but can migrate into the prostate veins and end up in the lungs!

For me, the idea of radiation treatment and implantation of seeds was not an option, primarily because it does not ensure success and, more importantly, from what all of the doctors say, once you have undergone this type of treatment, you are virtually foreclosed from the opportunity for a subsequent surgery intervention. Well, that's a hell of a chance to take. The cure rates for surgery and radiation are equal to ten years out. At fifteen years out, surgery starts to pull away as the most effective therapy.

On the other hand, if the patient is in their mid or upper 70s and, by the actuarial tables, has a life expectancy of only five to ten years, then they may not be a well-suited candidate for surgery. It may be better for them to try something less invasive, like perhaps the seeds.

The one thing I know for certain from my experience is, indeed, that everybody's case is different. Each patient has a different age, different physical conditioning, different mental stability, different PSA scores and changes, and different Gleason scores. There is no simple methodology by which one can say, okay, this is how it should be for everybody that has this formula or this combination. Although, I think it is safe to come away with a conclusion that if your PSA is relatively low—say less than four—and your biopsy Gleason Scores are less than 7, then surgery may not seem necessary. This patient may greatly benefit from dietary changes such as increasing their intake of lycopene from cooked tomato products and antioxidants from green tea. On the other hand, when you move up into the 7, 8, and above category, then you have to consider more serious treatments. If you're at an eight, nine or ten, you really just don't have much choice. At those levels, if the doctors think it is otherwise operative, I think surgery is absolutely mandatory. If, however, you're older and may not be able to tolerate the surgery, then perhaps they will choose radiation treatment in combination with hormone therapy to give you a few extra years. The side effects, the impact on incontinence and the impact on impotency are much the same, so the only benefit you would get by radiation treatment as an avoidance of surgery is exactly that - avoiding the surgery.

①		Glands are small, well-formed, and close together. There are only small signs of cancer.
②		Glands are larger and have more space in between them.
③		Glands are even further apart, are darker, and have different shapes.
④		There are hardly any glands. Cancer cells have lost their ability to form glands. Clumps of cancer cells throughout the tissue.
⑤		Often, there are no glands, there are sheets of cancer cells throughout the tissue.

ProstateCancer.net

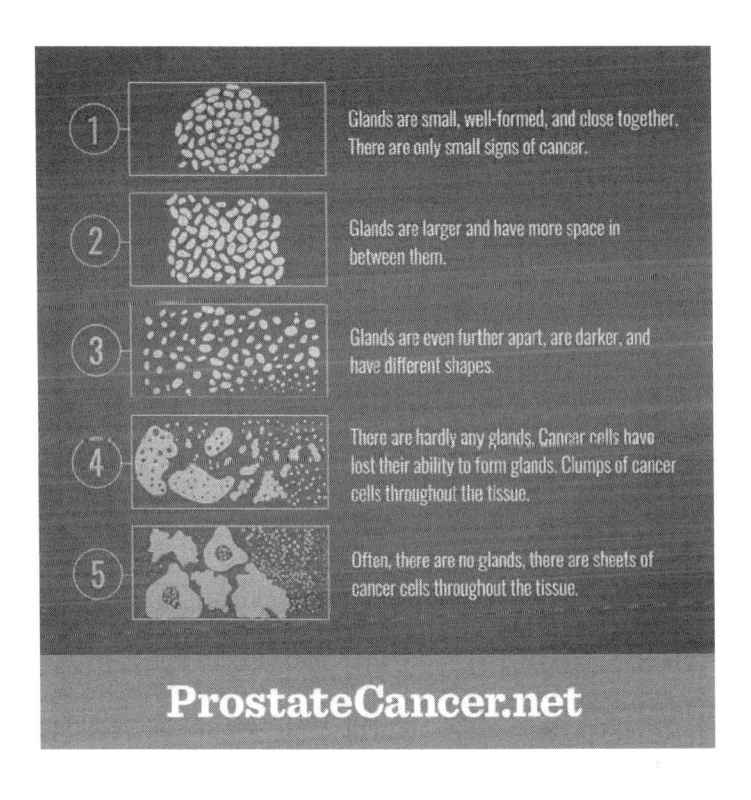

My Gleason Scores were six and seven. Seven is scary. That means the next step is local extension or metastasis. I did not want to take a chance on that because, once it gets there, options are very, very slim and life expectancy is traumatically impacted. My decision was easy. The decision I made was to have a radical prostatectomy.

9

Learning The Options

The day after Dr. Brady called and advised me, in fact, that six of the twelve biopsies were positive, he sent me to a seminar at the urology office. When Shirley and I got there, there were only two other couples, the weekly diagnostic catch, if you will, and a young doctor, one of the urologists from the group. He began to present to us a PowerPoint presentation program on a computer showing what is known as the DaVinci robotic laparoscopic procedure. Once we got there and learned that this was going to be the seminar, and while waiting for the doctor to get all of the equipment set up, I began reviewing one of the articles that they had in there about this process. Ignorance always being so ready at hand prompted me to disclaim, "I'll be damned if some robot is going to operate on me." I wanted the doctor to be able to see, feel and touch and do it right there. This was the first I had ever heard about this robotic surgery, and I sure as hell was not enthusiastic about some machine being all inside my abdomen and doing this process.

Well, I must say that an hour plus later, I was not so sure. I thought to myself, "Wow! This is amazing. Now I'm not so sure. Hmm. I wonder which is better." So, the pursuit of information continued. In laparoscopic surgery, the main surgeon sits at a console-like machine with his face up to a visual display screen cupped around his eyes and his hands' control knobs or levers, similar to a video game. The patient is on the operating table being attended to by another doctor and two surgical nurses fifteen feet away from the doctor operating the robot. In general and very simply, incisions are made in the naval, two on one side of the abdomen, another on the other side of the abdomen and a drain hole on that side of the abdomen as well. A camera is put inside, and the abdomen is inflated with carbon dioxide to create a workspace so the robotic surgical arms can go into the other incisions. The camera relays pictures from inside the patient's body to the TV screen, where the doctor watches the results of his finger movements as they are conveyed through the robotic arms to do the entire surgical procedure inside the abdomen. It's probably the damndest thing that you can imagine to see the first time; it was, at least for me. The doctor then, using the robotic surgical arms, does the cutting inside as he needs to, using "cold" scissors as well as electrical cauterization.

The steps to the procedure are as follows:

1. Drop the bladder from the anterior abdominal wall to expose the prostate.

2. Free up and then ligate (tie off) the dorsal vein, which is above the urethra as it passes out of the prostate and continues through the pelvic floor as it becomes the dorsal penile vein.

3. Separate the prostate from the bottom of the bladder. This is called the "bladder neck dissection" and technically can be the trickiest part of the operation because each prostate is shaped differently. The very large prostates that bulge into the bladder neck can be surgically challenging. Once the bladder neck is completely freed from the prostate, the bladder will

retract up in the pelvis, which allows for the seminal vesicles and both vas deferens to be removed from surrounding tissue and left attached to the prostate. At this point, the surgeon needs to gently lift the prostate off the prostate bed and leave the neurovascular bundles behind by using "cold" scissors, trying to avoid using cautery as this can "fry" the nerves.

4. Once both sides of the prostate are separated from the nerves, the only thing left to do is cut the previously tied-off dorsal vein so the urethra can be cut at the "apex" of the prostate.

5. Now that the prostate is completely free, a small silicone bag is delivered into the abdomen, opened, and the prostate is placed in the bag. By pulling on the string at the top of the bag, the prostate is completely bagged up and is pushed to the side for later removal.

6. The last step is sewing the hole in the bladder to the urethra. It usually takes about six to eight throws of stitches to complete a water-tight closure. A catheter is

inserted into the bladder, and then water is used to fill the bladder. At this point the surgeon is checking to see that the water that is put into the bladder does not leak into the abdomen.

7. The bag holding the prostate is then removed through the hole that the camera was in. Kind of like pulling a fish out of an ice hole! The Carbon Dioxide is evacuated from the abdomen; then all incisions are closed.

While there are several small incisions, cumulatively, they are dramatically less invasive than the normal procedure referred to as open surgery. In open surgery, the patient is cut open from the naval to the pubic bone. That's a lot of abdominal muscle to be cut and requires a lot of recovery time. In the open process, according to the statistics, the average blood loss is 950 to 1,000 ccs. Well, that's not a hell of a lot of blood in itself, and according to what the doctors say, this is not a real "bleeder" type of surgery like other more common surgeries of the body are. However, comparing 950 to 1,000 milliliters of blood loss in open surgery to an estimated blood loss of only 150 milliliters in robotic surgery, it's fairly dramatic. In other words, blood loss by DaVinci robotic surgery is about one-fifth (1/5) or less than that which occurs customarily in open surgery.

One result of this surgical process is that with your prostate gland gone, you do not have its restrictive control of the urethra and bladder, which controls your urination. We have different levels of control: the sphincter at the base of the bladder, the urinary and your pelvic floor sphincter. When you take out the prostate gland, urinary control will be lost, at least temporarily. So they have to put in a catheter which they insert through your penis up into the bladder, and there is a little balloon at the end of that catheter which is inflated and thereby acts somewhat as an anchor to hold that catheter in place. The catheter runs out of your penis, and you get to hook it to a bag for a period of time so that as urine is created in your bladder, it just runs right straight out into this bag. After all of the healing is done, or substantially done, the catheter is removed, and then you go into retraining to gain continence or control of your urine.

In the traditional open surgery procedure, the average time that the patient has to have this catheter is three weeks or longer. Compare that to robotic surgery, where the average catheter time is five to seven days. You can see again, a dramatic difference and great benefits of the robotic process.

I guess the part of it that convinced me the most, however, is the control and ability of the doctor. When you actually see the film on this process and look through the eye of the camera into the inside of the patient, it is remarkable. The vision for the surgery is enhanced by magnification many, many times. I'm not sure of that number, but I believe the doctors told me it was at least ten times magnification. Well, imagine a doctor standing over you physically on the surgical table; he can't see that well, even if he were to get down and put his nose in your cuts. So there's no question in my mind, and having seen it with my own eyes, that the magnification through the inserted camera gives the surgeon an absolutely incredibly increased ability to see all the structures and what he is doing. This is significantly important because amongst the things that need to be concerned about is avoiding injury to the nerves, or "nerve sparing."

There are two major nerves that run along the prostate gland that control such things as sexual function and urinary control, and it's very difficult for surgeons to effect a radical prostatectomy without injuring these nerves. Even when the nerves are spared, they are stretched during the procedure. For many months, the nerve suffers from neuropraxia or mild nerve damage. Think of when your leg falls asleep and feels numb but quickly recovers when you change the position or pressure that caused the numbness. With these tiny, microscopic nerves, the recovery can take a long time. If they can save at least one, then you have the ability to have a near-full recovery of your function. When I say that function, keep in mind that once you have a radical prostatectomy, there is never again any ejaculation. You can still have an orgasm, the same feeling, the same sensation or orgasm, but it's dry. The seminal vesicles have been removed.

So, nerve damage is a critical issue. No question by those who have compared and studied, and from what I have seen, that the best chance of nerve-sparing is through surgeon experience and expertise combined with the laparoscopic DaVinci robotic process.

10

The Robot

Well, after having read and learned all these things, you have to make a decision. If you have surgery, you will lose the ability to father children because you will no longer have any semen. There will be a dramatic impact on the ability to have an <u>erection</u>, at least for a period of time, either with or without assistance, and you will go through a period of <u>incontinence</u>. The question, really, though, is one of lifestyle and saving your life. For some people, younger, I guess, I'm told by the doctors that their number one priority is maintaining the ability to have children and just plain or basic sexual function. For me, that really does not rise to the same level as saving your life. Of course, maybe that's easier to say at age 61 than maybe for someone at age 40.

You need to make a decision. What kind of treatment will you opt for? Will it be just wait and see? Will it be radiation? Will it be the implantation of radioactive seeds? Or will it be surgery to remove the cancer? For me and my wife, the decision was simple. It really didn't even take any debate. Priority number one for us was to remove the cancer and thus increase the saving of life probability. Priority number two for me was to hope that the incontinence would not be a problem. That is, I would have a quick recovery in being able to control my bladder and urination and not have to effectively wear a diaper for life. Priority number three was for the restoration of sexual function, albeit without semen.

Therefore, with Gleason Scores of six and seven and not wanting to risk metastasization of going to an eight, it seemed clear to me that the almost certain decision would be surgery. Now the decision was, would it be the well-established success of the open surgery or the newer relatively–then only three years in this country–use of the laparoscopic DaVinci robotic process?

11

Bone Scan and A Decision

Before making the final decision, we had to know with as much certainty as possible whether or not my cancer had metastasized outside the prostate gland, thereby putting me in a much more life-threatening position of bone cancer or something else that would mandate radiation either with or prior to any other efforts.

This required me to have a bone scan. So we scheduled the bone scan as soon as possible, which was, I recall, about five days after the first announcement. The bone scan is really nothing. It's a matter of going to a radiology center where they inject some radioactive fluid into your body through your arm and let you rest, and then they put you in a machine that takes x-ray pictures of your whole body. If there are "hot spots," as they say, that means indications of cancer. According to the materials, cancer most often, if it has metastasized, will show up on the ribs and hip or legs of the patient.

Currently, bone scans or CT scans are rarely ordered. Many patients have had an MRI of their prostate and pelvis prior to their biopsy to target any regions of interest (ROI) at the time of biopsy. In 2005, however, bone scans were routine in checking for spreading cancer. They are not anymore.

Well, the only way I've ever known how to deal with a problem is to take it head-on. As I've sometimes said, "Damn enemies got me surrounded. That means I've got 'em exactly where I want 'em. I know where they are. I'm going to find my way out." That's gotten me through many, many years, from the military to practicing law as a trial lawyer over the last 50 years. Shirley and I intensified our research. She is on the computer, me with books and talking to doctors and friends. Soon after my bone scan, we took a trip. We went to New York City where I was optionally going to attend part of the National Association of Criminal Defense Lawyers Conference and also try to consult with doctors at the Sloan Kettering Clinic in Manhattan.

We went on to New York, and I was happy to see some of my friends from around the country. We get together usually four times a year at conferences in different locations from coast to coast. There are some who have become extremely close friends over the last many, many years, and I was happy just to be able to see them and talk to them again. I shared my predicament only because I didn't want them to find out later and be angry because I didn't tell them, much like holding back the information from my children. The concern clearly expressed on the faces of all who learned for our wellbeing was genuine. Shirley and I spent some of that time talking with them and visiting the Sloan Kettering Hospital Cancer Clinic in New York.

Well, when we got to the clinic, we found out what a damn zoo that place was. It was so basically "Helter Skelter in the Summer Swelter" that I just didn't want to have any damn thing to do with it. One thing I knew for sure was I wasn't going to put myself in that place to have any type of medical treatment done. You have to see it to imagine it, and perhaps that's the way hospitals in New York City are. Too busy and not enough seats even for the people in the reception area. No place to sit down and nobody to talk to.

Having done that, we were still awaiting the news of the bone scan. I'll never forget as we were walking up Madison Avenue looking for a couple of shops and a little previously unknown to us bistro for lunch–by the way, which we found every trip–I checked my cell phone messages, and there was one from my number one doctor, Charley Williams. He called to leave a message to tell me that he got the bone scan back, and it was all negative. A huge load immediately fell off my shoulders and those of my wife. We both were speechless and then began to smile. Shirley's response was, "Let's find a little restaurant and get some cake and a bottle of champagne, and when the waitress asks us what we're celebrating, I'll say, 'My husband's only got prostate cancer!'" We felt that was humorous, and we chuckled for a block, thinking how other people would look at that like, "What the hell is the matter with you? Are you insane?" But to us, it was wonderful news to have *only prostate cancer* with no metastatic disease whatsoever!

That made the decision-making process easier. I didn't have to worry about the spread of cancer at this point because it hadn't spread. Even though I had a seven on the Gleason Score, the bone scan was totally negative. We could reasonably, therefore, rely upon an almost medical certainty, certainly a probability, that the cancer had not spread and therefore, surgery would be predictably successful in removing all of the cancer. There was no guarantee, of course, and there's always a chance that something will happen between the day of the bone scan and the time of the surgery.

That raises another issue–how long do you wait? For me, there's no wait at all. That the only reasonable attack for me under my situation, my personal lifestyle, values, priorities, age, health, et cetera, was to have surgery and to have it as damned soon as I could. The rest of the world could just wait–my cases, my clients, my other problems–would just have to wait, and if they couldn't, God bless them. I was going to pay attention to ME. It was time to be selfish, to save my life and to have a longer life for me and my wife and my children, grandchildren and my friends from around the world.

Back at the conference, we shared the news of the non-spreading of the cancer with our friends and had a little celebration. The next step was to get home, meet with the doctor to make the final decisions, and then start trying to implement them. We met with my primary urologist. He asked if we had made the decision. I told him that I had and I explained my reasons, and I observed his smile of reassuring agreement. While doctors don't want to tell you what your decision should be or to do, rather only advise you much like us lawyers, it was very clear that I had made the right decision in the mind and judgment of my doctor. I was going to have surgery, and I wanted it soon.

Now the question was, do I have open surgery or robotic? I was certainly leaning towards robotic surgery based on all of the things I had read, but I still wanted to hear other experts compare the two processes before making the decision.

Fortunately, in my career, I've come to meet some wonderful people. One of them was a dear friend of mine from Miami, Don Russo, who was a renowned personal injury and malpractice lawyer who had also done other types of civil litigation for years and years. Don made the arrangements for us to see Dr. Wajsman in Gainesville who was the head of the urology department. We talked with him on a special appointment, and he did the exam–Mr. KY again—and confirmed that the surgical process he would opt for is the laparoscopic DaVinci robotic procedure. He said that if he were going to have it done on himself, it would be at the Florida Hospital in Orlando, done by a doctor from Winter Park Urology, Dr. Jeffrey Thill. What an amazing sense of comfort and relief that brought to Shirley and me. That was the very doctor, the very group, the very hospital that I had been talking to. Dr. Thill was a partner of my primary urologist, who does not do the robotic surgery. Indeed, Dr. Thill was remembered by the Chief of Urology at Shands as being the best resident he ever had and this young fellow had been gone from there a dozen years. Dr. Wajsman also said that in that calendar year alone, then at the beginning of May, he had referred five patients to Dr. Thill for this process, all of whom reported great success and satisfaction, and more compelling, all of whom were themselves doctors.

This helped us again to be very confident in the decision-making process. Hell, we'd already made arrangements to go anywhere in the world that would be the best. I had another client, a long-term client and friend for over 30 years, an extremely successful businessman– who owned a 33 million-dollar Gulf Stream jet airplane. He offered it to me to go wherever I needed to go to have this surgical process. All I needed to do was call him, and no matter the schedule, hour, or day, the pilots would be ready and at my disposal to take the plane anywhere. What a comforting situation that was because the most notorious places working with the DaVinci robotic process were places like John Hopkins and the Cleveland Clinic. The machinery itself was invented in Paris. My client told me, "Hell, take it to Paris if you want to; it is only seven hours, wheels up from Orlando to wheels down at Charles de Gaulle Airport non-stop." So I was armed and ready.

With Dr. Wajsman's endorsement, why would I want to go gallivanting around, fancy private Gulf Stream or not, if I could do it right here at home? Traveling had been one of my main concerns. I didn't want to have to go through a commercial airport, first class or not, with a damn urine bag hanging on a catheter strapped to my leg or in my hand. How humiliating as well as dangerous and uncomfortable that may be. I much preferred to be at home with my wife and have her friends and her mother and all of my friends around, rather than being out of the country or out of town to do this. Things were starting to look pretty good.

I now knew that I could look forward to the surgery that was highly endorsed as rendering the least invasive, greatest chance of recovery, right here at home. All we had to do now was get Dr. Thill's schedule. So, I told my primary doctor that the decision was absolutely made, and we were done; get me on the list. Sign me up.

We were faced with a new problem. There was only one such robotic machine in the hospital, and it had to be shared amongst the various different urology groups in the area. I had hoped that once I said I wanted this done, I would be able to have the surgery within two weeks. Well, it turned out I had to wait six weeks. I told them to put me on a standby list. I was ready at any given time should somebody cancel or change their mind. If the time opened up, give me a call, I'll be there in an hour. Or, in reality, a day and a half later, giving Mr. Fleets time for the clean-out process.

12

Preparing For Surgery

Nevertheless, hope against hope, we held out that maybe there would be a cancellation, that maybe there would be an opportunity; maybe somebody could help by saying, look, here's somebody who wants to get it done right away, and we move ahead. But that didn't happen. The extra time did allow me to prepare physically for the surgery. The books and the doctors told me that vigorous exercise and really getting in good physical shape would be one of the most important things that I could do for myself prior to the operation. I took them seriously.

I've always been in reasonably good physical shape, particularly for someone with a sedentary-type profession and my age. Shirley and I tried to power walk every day. Weather interventions and scheduling conflicts made that reality four or five days a week. Our walks were generally three miles, sometimes longer, at about a 4 mph pace. That's a pretty vigorous exercise for about 45 minutes and, therefore, kept me in generally good shape. To prepare for surgery, I added a whole regimen. Now, every morning, I did a half hour of various abdominal exercises, including traditional calisthenics, leg lifts, crunches, Kegel exercises, and using an abdominal wheel. After the full 30/40 minutes of abdominal exercise, the same amount of time with free weights, then the power walk. This was now my job. My job is to take care of myself and get ready for surgery. To hell with clients and cases. I wiped them out and took them off the board. I now went to work at the crack of 11 to see what I could do over a few hours each day! At least the exercise cleared my mind enough to concentrate and not commit malpractice. So, for the next six weeks, that's what I did. Every single day. Two hours a day of exercising and getting in shape. Believe it or not, in that short period of time, I really saw some results. My stomach was flattening and getting strong, getting ready for the process, and my whole body was strong. I cannot tell you how important I think good physical conditioning before surgery is to the recovery period. Kegel exercises are one of the most important parts of the conditioning prior to prostate surgery.

Of course, now with a concerted plan all laid out, I am clear in what I'm doing; I'm having robotic surgery; we're scheduling as soon as possible; I know who's doing it, where it is being done; I'm in good shape; I know the process; I know what to anticipate. Now, I can really start focusing solely on the recovery; that is, of course, once we get to the procedure and get it over with.

Being reminded of the abdominal muscle pain as a result of surgery. I was intent on ensuring that I could do everything possible to lessen those difficulties with this procedure. The doctors are clear: there's no substitute for making exercise a top priority. I'm not talking about just a little exercise or feeling like you have earned your glass of wine–I'm talking about a dedicated couple of hours of full exercise. Doing the abdominal exercises, the weight training and the power walk is a pretty good full-body workout. Certainly, it would not be something set for those people who want to be Arnold Schwarzeneggers or other bodybuilders, but conditioning is unsurpassed as a requirement and a necessary preparation for surgery.

Now, the word spread amongst friends and colleagues that, indeed, I had cancer and was awaiting this major surgery. It was astounding the number of people who had a friend or relative who had been through this in years past. Although I did not know of anyone personally who had gone through the robotic surgery, I knew numerous people who had preceded me with the surgery in the open process. Interestingly, I can't tell you the number of folks who called me to make sure that I knew the name of the doctor that they were certain was the most expert in the world. There are so many of them that it is amazing and, therefore, a great compliment to the medical profession. It seems that every person who has been through the surgery and survived will tell you with their last breath that their doctor was the best in the world, and you needed to see or get that person to do it. I had that identified "best doctor in the world" given to me by at least eight different friends, all of whose judgment I greatly value. There were the world famous doctors, one in Miami, one that was in Orlando, one that was out in the Midwest now up at Northwestern University Teaching Hospital in Chicago, the famous Dr. Walsh of Johns Hopkins, and on and on. Each of these fellows has successfully operated on literally hundreds of prostate cancer victims and saved their lives. They are phenomenal doctors with reputations that have been clearly well-earned. Unfortunately, each and every one of them performed the open procedure, and none had yet been trained in or had the DaVinci robotic procedure.

With the benefit of time, we recognize the advances that are being made in the surgical process. Three years prior to my diagnosis, the DaVinci robotic surgery was not known and was not done in the United States at all. The open surgery process was all that there was, and these fellows became the best at it. I'm sure that around the country, there are bound to be hundreds of urologists who are absolutely perfect in their job of performing the open surgery processes. Now, not only do we have robotic surgery, which promises to be much less invasive than the open surgical process and predictably with better outcomes, but we also have advances to help post-surgical recovery, especially dealing with the issue of impotency. Five years before my surgery, we didn't have Viagra or Cialis. The only assistance medically that was available to help the post-surgical recovery of erection function was shooting a drug into the penis with a needle. That never sounded like a hell of a lot of fun to me. I can't imagine the circumstances of how you would have a sexual mood and "Excuse me, I've got to take this hypodermic needle to myself." Obviously, thousands of men did so with their wives and partners and were able to deal with it quite effectively. Happily, that process is history. In a very short period of time, the side effects of impotency were greatly reduced by the advent of the availability of the drugs Viagra, Cialis and perhaps others and then a new surgical process that would sweep the world as more and more doctors become trained in its use. The myriad of benefits of the DaVinci robotic surgery process, including the much smaller incision, reduced blood loss, reduced time requiring the use of the Foley catheter and urine bag, and the possibility of nerve sparing were dramatic improvements.

In addition to the necessary physical conditioning, there are mental hurdles to conquer when preparing for surgery. A strange thing happened to me as I looked mortality in the eye (something that I have not shared before this writing). Over the last several days prior to the surgery; I would have daydreams or even full dreams at night of visions of family members and friends and people that I had known that passed away over the last many, many years. People that I had not thought about in maybe ten years who had died prematurely would enter my mind in various situations, their faces and voices clear. This includes my parents, my grandparents, aunts and uncles, friends, people from the military, people from bar associations, and others. When I first became aware of this, I started getting a little afraid. What did this mean? Was it some sort of mystical premonition? Were these folks ready to welcome me aboard? Or was my mind just playing tricks on me? Yes, there is the possibility any time a person is under general anesthesia, especially for a prolonged period of time and undergoing surgery that, they might not come out of it. I discussed this with my wife on several occasions, telling her that I had a little concern or fear about not waking up but that I was no longer fearful about it, kind of in the biblical sense, "O death, where is thy sting?" I didn't want it. I wasn't ready for it. I didn't want my wife and daughters to be faced with the repercussions of my untimely death, but could I let that fear keep me from having the surgery? No! I was not going to sit around and wait for the cancer to eat me up and put me through a painful death and the long rigors of medical treatment. The only option was to get on with the surgery.

My doctor and his entire team distributed a list of things to do and not do prior to surgery. That information sheet provided:

14 Days Prior to Surgery

STOP taking any aspirin products, Plavix or any blood thinners, as these may increase your chance of excess bleeding during surgery.

STOP taking any ibuprofen or related non-steroidal anti-inflammatory drugs.

STOP taking all herbal supplements, including vitamin E, two weeks before surgery.

STOP taking supplements that act as blood thinners, which increase the chance of excessive bleeding during surgery, including ginkgo biloba, garlic, gensing, dong quai, willow, and red clover.

Seven Days Prior to Surgery

If you have been prescribed Coumadin or Warfarin, call the doctor who prescribed them and ask if it is okay to STOP taking them in light of your impending surgery. While it is generally beneficial to stop these seven days prior to surgery, in certain cases, it is not advisable. If your doctor does NOT allow you to discontinue taking these, please inform your surgeon.

Two Days Prior to Surgery

Absolutely avoid consuming any alcohol or alcoholic beverages forty-eight hours prior to surgery and forty-eight hours after surgery. These can have disastrous consequences on the surgery as well as the anesthesia.

The Day Before Surgery

Absolutely do not take any medications or supplements already stopped (above), including aspirin or ibuprofen.

Follow a clear, liquid diet with lots of water. Do not take any milk products.

Take the bowel evacuant as directed. You can purchase this at any drugstore. You do not need a prescription.

Very Important

Stay on a clear, liquid diet the whole day prior to your surgery. Start Fleet Prep Kit (bowel evacuant) at 12:00 noon the day before.

The six weeks of waiting for my surgery date were coming to an end. I was as physically ready as I could possibly be. The weeks of daily rigor had paid off, and I was in the best physical shape that I had been in, probably 15 or 20 years. I had faced and overcome my fears. I had stopped taking supplements. It was time for the surgery.

13

The Day Of Surgery

On the day before surgery, you're treated to what's known as the Fleets Pack 1. A delightful process. Starting at noon, you drink a soda, if you will, of Fleet's chemicals. It comes in a little small bottle that is diluted with water or juice. Juice is the best at covering the taste. You drink three eight-ounce glasses of this mixture within 20 minutes. That's no big deal, and frankly, it didn't taste all that bad. You just slug it down, and there it is. This begins the clean-out process, so you will need to stay close to a toilet. Four hours later, you take pills that carry on additional laxative processes and then finally, in the evening, when you go to bed, a suppository that you endeavor to hold in place by your sphincter control for at least 15 to 20 minutes before you have the last bowel movement for clean-out. This really is not that bad a process, and when you know how important it is, it's just something that you do. You're getting ready to go to the hospital, to be put out, operated on and come home, so just get it done and don't whine about it. Fleets Pack works pretty damn well. From midnight on, you are 100% fasting so that when you go to the hospital the next morning, there's nothing in you. No water, no juice, no coffee, nothing. Total fasting after a total clean out.

On the day of surgery, you may and probably should take any of certain currently prescribed medications, including heart medication, blood pressure medication, anti-seizure medication, and one-half of a normal dose of insulin. Do not take water pills or diabetic pills in addition to anything you have previously stopped during the preparation process. If you have accidentally taken any medication or supplements or eaten food that you should not have, please advise your doctor immediately. Bring all medications currently prescribed to you in their labeled containers with you to the hospital. As with all hospitalizations, you should leave non-essential valuables (such as watches, jewelry, and phones) at home to reduce the chance of misplacing or losing them in the hospital. If you wear glasses, contact lenses, false teeth, hearing aids, or related personal items, remember to bring a case to store them in during the surgery.

I've never known why, but it seems to me that all doctors like to start early. We were told to be at the hospital at 5 a.m. in the morning. That meant leaving my house at quarter after 4 a.m. to ensure there would be no traffic difficulties or delays. That meant getting up at 3 or 3:15 a.m. for my wife so that she could try to organize herself dealing with her normal routines as well as her enhanced anxiety. We had asked friends to drive us, which I highly recommend. You can't drive yourself going in there to face this battle, and your wife is likely to have far too much anxiety to do so. So get a friend to come pick you up and drive you to the hospital.

We arrived at the hospital, indeed, almost exactly at 5 a.m. to be taken right into the pre-screening room, where they simply confirmed that, yes, I still had insurance. Of course, we had gone to the hospital three days before this, where they took yet another photocopy of my insurance card and also my American Express card to pre-pay for some amount of the hospital stay. After checking it again, we were directed into the waiting room with the other folks who were awaiting surgery for various maladies that morning. Shortly after arriving in that part, I was taken into a room where blood was drawn for testing and was then moved on to the pre-operation preparation room. Here, the nurse installed the intravenous equipment and paraphernalia in the back of my hand to be used for the administration of drugs.

After a little wait, the doctor who would be on duty in the operating room as the anesthesiologist came to introduce himself, ask questions about my prior surgical experiences and talk generally about the process. He was very informative, and I appreciated him. The one thing, however, that we did not talk about and is one of the reasons why I'm taking the trouble to write all of this is there was no discussion about exactly how long he thought I would be under anesthesia or what impact the anesthesia might have on me. I knew from talking to my surgeon that the expected surgical process would be between three and three and one-half hours, followed by the normal recovery time of an estimated hour. I learned the hard way that many folks experience a great deal of nausea after prolonged anesthesia. One does not want to be nauseous and have a vomiting attack after having abdominal surgery. You can imagine that. So, I'm telling you to discuss the possibility of nausea with your surgeon and the anesthesiologist in advance and be prepared to deal with it.

At any rate, as I lay there in this curtained-off part of the staging room, I expected someone to shave me, but they didn't. I expected someone to give me a pill or some drug, but they didn't. The next thing I knew, I was being wheeled out into yet another pre-surgery room where they started doing those things. Shortly thereafter came the needle to administer the drugs into my IV port. Actually, I don't even remember them doing that. That's the high value of the drug Versed. It is used in combination with others to prevent pain. It also prevents memory of what is going on. In reality, the next thing I remember is coming to the recovery room with my lifetime friend standing next to me.

After some sporadic, disjointed conversation, I was wheeled to my hospital room. The only part of that I remember is the orderly pushing me and my declaring with increasing urgency how violently I needed to pee. "I've got to pee. Stop. I've got to pee! I've got to pee!"

Well, of course, I didn't and couldn't because the catheter was in place, and I was already hooked to a bag. But

I can tell you that the sensation, the pressing urgency, was unbelievable. At any rate, they got me into the room, and very shortly thereafter, I was asleep.

At some point, not too long, I suspect, my surgeon came in to see me and talk to me and my wife. I guess he had already talked to her about it but explained to me that the surgery had been a good bit more extensive and complicated than they had anticipated. This was because the mesh installed during the hernia surgery four years earlier had caused a problem. The mesh, designed to hold the intestines in place and not allow them to be herniated, had itself adhered to some of the intestines, as well as the bladder. That meant for the surgeon to be able to do his otherwise normal robotic process, he had to clean up the adhesions and cut away and get rid of the scar tissue areas there so he could have full access. Apparently, that took an extra 45 minutes before he could get to the real process. The impact of that was, of course, to make the surgical process itself more extensive but also to extend the period of time which I was compelled to be under general anesthesia. This always enhances the risk and the recovery side effects. Nevertheless, he reported that it was quite successful. An additional complication was that my prostate gland was a good bit larger than they had anticipated. This meant that they had to cut the incision, crossing vertically up and down over my naval to be about twice as big as they otherwise had anticipated. Remember, this is where the fish comes out of the ice hole. So, they had to make the opening bigger in order to pull the parts out.

Between the unexpected extra 45 minutes of surgical procedure to clear up the adhesions from the hernia mesh and then the re-incision to make the opening to remove the prostate gland, the time that I was first anesthetized prior to the surgery, then through the surgery and into the recovery room, was pushing seven hours. I'm sure that this caused a good deal of concern for my wife and friends who were standing by. Me—hell—I didn't know anything about it. Everything was fine.

I came to; there we were, and I was learning about all the stuff hanging on me. I had forgotten that there would be a catheter inserted and a bag hanging off of it. Also, they have to put a drain on my abdomen. That sounds great, doesn't it? Well, this is to drain the blood from the surgical site, and actually, it's a pretty simple process. They inject a tube-like needle, similar to a meat thermometer in size, into the lower right abdomen, and I believe, as I saw it actually come out, it is about a five or six-inch long weapon. It's hooked to what they call a ball, a collecting process. It looks like it would probably hold about a 1/4 of a cup, maybe more. So that was stuck in my side and hanging there, along with the rest of these incisions. I was told that it was just to collect the drainage, and sometime during the night, one of the nurses came in and took that collector out, emptied it and put it back. The needle-like tube stayed in place. No big deal.

At this point, I had not been able to eat for a couple of days. After fasting and the clear liquid diet for the entire day before surgery, the Fleets Pack, nothing on the day of surgery, and now coming out of the fog, I was feeling hungry, but quite frankly, not really wanting to eat. They brought me juice, Jello, and broth at their scheduled time as my first meal. One of the things that we learned through our reading was that, in general, you're not supposed to eat things like red Jell-O, cherry, strawberry and the like, or drink grape juice or anything that's red. This is because the dye may tend to obscure the true color of the urine and, therefore, reveal detections of blood.

For whatever reason, the dietician in the hospital and/or the serving nurse didn't understand that, so when they brought me red Jell-O and some sort of red fruit juice, we had to tell them, no, I can't have that. I guess everybody learns something at some time, and it didn't take too long before they learned that we were right and changed everything. Of course, again, I wasn't hungry anyway. I had no idea that I needed to eat, but I would do what I was told. So I took some broth and some other colored Jell-O and water.

The first night, in fact, the only night in the hospital, was somewhat uneventful. The nurse would come in and check the drain tube on my side, go into that little cup, drain the urine bag, and ask some inane questions. I just wanted to be left alone to sleep.

The process was expected to have me going home the next day. I had told the doctors and the hospital people not to rush me; that if I felt like I wanted to stay, then I'd stay, and I didn't give a damn about the insurance paying for it; I'd pay for it myself if need be. But my doctor wanted me out of there as he said, "The sooner you're out of the hospital, the better I like it," because it reduces the chance of infection. Alright, I could go along with that. So the next mid-morning, the doctor came in; he looked over the suture areas, pulled off all of the bandages and made his "ums" and "uh-huhs" and so forth and then said he was going to remove the drain. I remembered my friend telling me that when he got his drain removed—which, by the way, was by the same doctor—it was quite a process and to be prepared for it. There was hardly anything in the little collector bulb when the guy came in and proceeded to pull it out. At this point, I thought the damn thing was two feet long; it just kept going, going and going, but in truth, while it was an annoyance, it wasn't greatly painful. It was certainly something that could be tolerated. They don't even sew that up; they just let that hole close naturally. They put a bandage over it, a big gauze pad to continue to absorb whatever came out of it, and that was that. The bandages on the rest of the sutures were left off. I had some more Jell-O and some rest. My wife was there the entire time, and other friends came to visit. The doctor wanted me up and out of bed, so around noon, they helped me move over to sit in a chair. This was about 24 hours after the surgery was over.

Sitting in the chair, I was not feeling too badly at all. Quite frankly, the incision areas were numb. The only one that seemed to be a little sensitive was the extended cut through the naval. After resting in a chair for a while and having another visitor, it was time to give it a try. They wanted me to walk. As soon as I could walk around the entire perimeter of the hallway on that ward, I would be ready to go home.

Well, we got up there and did it. My wife walked with me, and the nurse followed. I held the bag of urine and walked around the damn hospital. It wasn't bad at all, quite frankly, and it was easier than I thought it might be, and apparently, I walked faster than they had any reason to expect I could. I guess some of that conditioning was starting to pay off. At any rate, the walk was completed without event, and then we were back in the room to await the processing and final checks and inspections. Of course, there was a wheelchair ride to the car. My friend picked us up again, driving us to take us home. In a very short period of time, I was back in my own house and on the bed. This is another problem. It was wonderful to be home, wonderful to be there, even though I had only been gone a day and a half. I was home by 4:00 in the afternoon and had left at 4:00 the morning before. A day and a half and I was back in my own bed.

14

Going Home

Being back in my own bed was wonderful, but it did reveal a new problem. With all of these incisions in my abdomen, I couldn't raise and lower myself. I couldn't sit up, and I was too big for my wife to be able to manage me. Another good friend and neighbor—the fellow who was a former football player and a whole lot younger than me—came over and put his arms around my chest and back and lifted me up so that my wife could get pillows under me and I could be in reasonable comfort. And I was. On that first night at home, Saturday night, for the most part, I slept through the night.

I'm sure my wife didn't sleep much as she listened to every moan, groan, sound and sigh, but nevertheless, it was a pretty uneventful night. The next day, however, turned out to be a whole lot different.

On Sunday morning, as I awoke and was given some juice, some Jell-O and some water, I really wasn't feeling particularly good. I wasn't in pain, mind you. The incisions did not hurt. The catheter did not hurt. All of that part of my body was numb.

But I just wasn't feeling good in my stomach. By about noon, I started feeling very, very nauseous, and I thought I was going to throw up. Knowing I had nothing to vomit to begin with, I became more and more curious, but the intensity increased and increased until finally, I began vomiting nothing. My wife, her mother, and my friends rushed to try to help. I cannot tell you how painful it is to be retching, going into dry heaves, with five incisions in your abdomen. There had been some coughing the night before and in the hospital recovery room, where the nurses showed me a trick to help that. That is, to hold a pillow firmly against your abdomen with both hands as to, I guess, disburse the pressure or hold it in so it doesn't hurt so much, whatever; it damn sure works a great deal in relieving the pain of just an ordinary cough.

So trying to hold a pillow, somebody trying to hold my head and retching, was just horrifying. There is no other word to describe it except horrifying. My wife tried immediately to get in touch with the doctor's on-call people, but without success. After some period of time and about my third round of this violent retching, she was able to get the doctor who called in a prescription for emergency medicine to fight nausea. Lucky for us, the nearby Walgreens is only a couple of minutes away, so she, or somebody else, was able to get some nausea medicine that is used sublingually. That is, the small pill, Zofran, was put under my tongue for immediate blood absorption. It worked. Before getting it, however, was indeed the most painful and worst day of my life. The only thing that was being produced by the dry heave retching and vomiting was bile. Pure green bile. My arms and hands were tingling and going numb; I felt like I was going in and out of consciousness, and quite frankly, at that point in time, I thought, "Oh my God." Those visions and faces that I had seen were calling me on board after all. This can't be right. I'm not going to sit here and die from some damn complications from surgery after the surgery has been successful!

The Zofran was like a miracle. It took effect, the nausea subsided, and I slept. About this time, my good friends Larry and Alice, who were with us through the whole process, came up with a solution to the problem of lifting me on and off the bed. They made a few calls and were able to get an emergency delivery of a hospital bed. I was able to get up off of my regular bed and onto the hospital bed, where the elevation was easily controlled with the touch of a button. There is no substitute for being able to have a power lift to change your body position without straining and using those invaded abdominal muscles. What a remarkable relief that was! Both of these problems could have been avoided. Whether or not your doctor mentions these issues, my message to you is, do not leave the hospital without a prescription for medicine to combat nausea and have a hospital bed or a reclining bed in place before going home.

15

Catheter

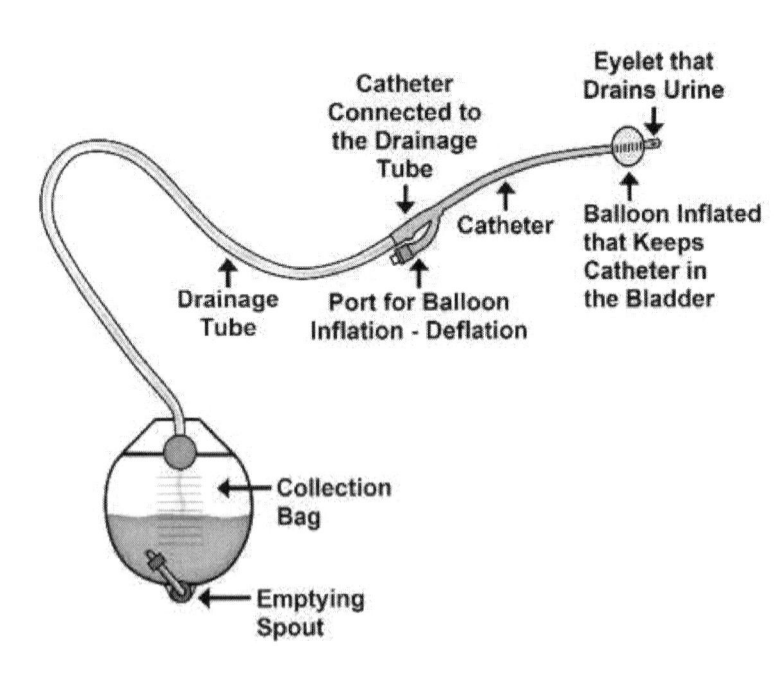

If you read the various instructions for pre-operation care and post-operation care provided by most urologists and oncologists, they will reveal the fact that there is going to be a catheter. Unfortunately, they don't tell you what the hell a catheter is or, more importantly, what it really is.

First, there is the Foley catheter itself. This is a plastic tube of silicone or coated latex—a strong tube that is inserted through the end of your penis and runs all the way up to your bladder. The tube has two separate channels running down its length. One channel is open at both ends and drains urine. The other channel has a valve on the outside end and connects to a balloon at the inside tip. They then inflate the balloon, and it acts as an anchor. As it comes out of your penis then, there is an eight or ten-inch segment of the tube that has another little "Y" off of it with a cap. This is for the inflation of the balloon as well as for later taking it out. The main end of the tube, however, has a flange-like fitting on the end of it, which is where the hose and the bag are attached. That portion, at the end of the actual catheter, will be secured to your leg.

This is an interesting contraption. They have a big plastic adhesive bandage with two hooks on it, similar to picture hanging wall hooks, except made out of plastic with a little locking grip on it, which reminds me somewhat of plastic handcuffs. The tube goes through those hooks and is fastened down so that it holds it in place. This means that no matter what really happens to you, you're not going to move your leg the wrong way and pull that damn thing out. So from that end of your penis, then, they have this loop which puts some slack in the tube to where it then is affixed to your leg. It goes on past that a few more inches, as I said, to the flange fitting, where you then push in the fitting from the tube for the collection bag. The tube itself appears to be 3/8 inch in diameter—I don't know what the interior opening is, obviously smaller than that—and is about five feet long. That drains into a bag that has a one-way valve on it so that the bladder then drains straight through the urethra catheter into the bag and fills up. This bag will hold about 1,000 ccs and usually will need to be drained at about 400 or 500 ccs. It's a pretty neat device. The bottom of the bag has a drain tube that has a clip on it that is simply pushed closed so there can be no leakage, then above that is just a clip-on, like a quick-release fastener that holds it in place on the bag. So when it's time to empty the bag, you just unclip that end of it, hold that into the measuring drain cup they provide you, then undo the closing clip, and it just drains right out.

Of course, this is not something you can do by yourself, at least for several days. Your stomach will still be quite sore and you will not be able to bend over, so your wife or someone else to help you is absolutely essential. Someone has to get that bag positioned over the collecting cup, unsnap the closure clip, drain it, then close the bag and put it back where it was. Another interesting thing: you have to deal with gravity. You can't have this bag level with you; it needs to be down below where you are in the bed. You could just lay it on the floor and hope that nobody steps on the damn things because I don't know how good that one-way valve is. If somebody steps on it, it might shoot it back up, and I can assure you that would be enormously painful.

They also provide a different form of collector bag, a smaller one. They say this is for shorter times. That is strapped to your leg just above the knee and down below the knee with a shorter tube that goes into the collection flange that's fastened to your thigh. I tried it a couple of times, and it's okay, but it fills fairly quickly, and it's more awkward to drain. It doesn't have the two-stage control clips on it like the big bag does. They tell you one way you can drain it is to just stand in the shower, pull the end of that collection bag open, and let it empty on your leg, foot and in the shower. That certainly would be okay, depending on how often you were going to be standing in the shower. Of course they want you to do that a couple of times a day at least, but that wouldn't be enough time to drain that bag. Frankly, after trying it, I found it was easier to endure the whole process by just leaving the big bag and long hose connected. When you get up to walk, you can carry it with you and then wherever you sit down, lay it on the floor or preferably something to hang it on, like basically using a walker. That's what I did because it made it easier to get in and out of the bed and just hang that bag on the bottom rung of the walker and it goes where you want it to.

What they don't tell you about this catheter process is how impossible it makes it to sleep. I want you to envision now that you have this catheter run up into your middle insides, out your penis, strapped to your leg, going to a 5-foot hose and a bag. You can't turn over on your side—either side—because it'll pull the bag and the hose. It also is very uncomfortable because of the surgery itself to do anything other than lay on your back and try to sleep.

The reality is for at least the first week after the surgery, you're going to have this catheter. Unfortunately for me, I had to have it an extra five days because of the unplanned nausea and resulting ripping of the internal stitches where the bladder was re-sewed to the urethra.

Under normal circumstances, if you follow my suggestions and insist on the damn medicine to fight nausea before you leave the hospital and have a hospital/reclinable bed so you don't have to strain so much in trying to lay down or sit up, you should be able to get the catheter out in only one week. You should count on a full week of being in bed, and when you are in bed, having to simply lay on your back.

During the last few days of my twelve days with the catheter, I noticed leaking from my penis even though that damned hose stuck in there all the way up into the bladder was supposed to be collecting all the urine. I talked to the doctor about it and learned that it was a product of a bladder spasm. It is the most compellingly urgent need to urinate that you have felt perhaps in your life, but you can't do it. It's just the pain, the excruciating urge, and then the uncontrolled leaking and dribbling. You can't start it, and you can't stop it. You will be advised not to attempt to do any of the Kegel exercises while the catheter is in place. For me, the last four days, which I remind you were over time due to the nausea-related problems, were pretty testy. I would have these tremendous urges and resulting pressure in my penis just about every time I stood up, and all I could do was just stand there somewhat paralyzed until the spasm passed. It is for that reason that, the last few days, I started wearing the Depends diapers so that the leaking and dribbling from the end of my penis around the catheter tube would be captured rather than going on the floor or in the bed.

I think the experience with the catheter was one of the most trying of the entire process. I'm going to try to ignore the uncontrolled nausea, vomiting and the problems that it caused because I know that was abnormal and should not have occurred. In an ordinary situation, which I hope is all that you have to experience, you will deal with the recovery from the stomach incisions and the catheter. Apparently, in my situation, the nausea was related to the substantial involvement of my doctor having to deal with intestinal adhesions from a prior hernia surgery. Some patients with even worse adhesions had no nausea. Others who have had very successful surgeries have later had to be readmitted to the hospital for nausea, even though they did not have the same complications in the process. It apparently is not so totally predictable, therefore reinforcing my insistence on having the Zofran available.

What they also don't tell you about this most invasive and insulting process is the removal of the catheter. I don't know how to really explain the process other than to say to you that hose going up your penis, you would never have expected to be able to fit, to begin with. How in the world they do that, I'll never know. But, when it comes out, this is another whole drill.

You go back to the doctor and after checking out and inquiring and so on and so on, they start the process. The first thing is that through that second Y-shaped part of the catheter that is strapped to your leg, the attendant nurse or physician's assistant does something to deflate the balloon. I saw him with a big syringe that went somewhere, and I knew it didn't go into my body. I believe it went into that Y valve, and it may have simply extracted the air from the balloon, but I sure felt that dull "thump, thump" inside. Strange feeling, not sharp pain, but a dull, surprising kind of pain. Perhaps it's not even best to describe it as a pain, just a sensation, but clearly not pleasant. I guess it's kind of like thumping yourself in the naval.

When that was done, the doctor told me to take a deep breath and relax, whereupon he had already gripped that catheter by the end of my penis and started pulling it straight out. It felt like it was five feet long rather than only eight or ten inches. It seemed like he pulled for a long, long time, though, in truth, it was not painful. It was just a very strange, dull and unpleasant sensation, but then it was gone. Immediately there was an uncontrolled draining of urine, now straight from my penis and not into the catheter or collection bag. This underscored the need for Depends because there was no bladder control at all.

Being finally free of the catheter is a huge step in recovery! However, I did experience phantom sensations of the catheter for the next several days. It felt like it was still there when it wasn't. There was also a little bit of bleeding, as one might imagine from the irritation of the hose being stuck in you like that, but it was insignificant. The next issue to deal with was the lack of bladder control. The constant leaking, dribbling of urine, and wearing the Depends, what I call diapers.

The doctors advise you to start doing the Kegel exercises again as soon as you can after the catheter is removed, and I took them at their word. Just as in the weeks preparing for surgery, I was back to tightening for ten, then releasing for ten all day long. I also had to get used to wearing that diaper, which got heavier by the hour. Of course, it was somewhat humiliating, but in reality, who the hell cares? Anybody that's had this surgery has done it, and those who haven't had it yet are going to, so big deal. At least, that's what I told myself to make it bearable.

I found that in the first several days, a change of the Depends was required every two or three hours. I also advise getting right in the shower and hosing off because even though they are a great product, you still have urine around your groin, your testicles, your hips and so forth. I liked to wash off at least a couple of times a day, dry, and then step right into the Depends again.

What a great relief it is to have the catheter gone and, like a smiling baby, have on a fresh, dry pair of Depends! It is also a relief to get rid of the hospital bed and get back in your own, where you can actually move around, albeit somewhat gingerly, without being tied to the catheter and the drain bag. Now you can turn on your side. Of course, you're not going to lay on your stomach for some time. I found that in the early days of freedom, turning on my side, while it was a relief for my back, caused some discomfort in my stomach because of the weakness of the area. Straightening my legs out seemed to relieve some of that pressure, whereas a more fetal position was somewhat stressful to the lower abdomen. At any rate, the freedom to move was very helpful in trying to sleep. The only thing interfering with my sleep now was the damned diaper filling up.

I found after about the third day on the diaper that during the night, I would be cognizant of the sensation of needing to urinate. I tried to get out of bed and get to the bathroom so that I could try to urinate in the toilet rather than in the diaper. The first few times of this were pretty tricky because I had virtually no control. The urine flowed almost unrestricted, so I had to learn to get myself positioned over the toilet so that when the diaper came down, I was positioned to hit the toilet and not the seat. After just a few tries, I became pretty expert at that.

It was a great relief to appreciate the fact that I had some control; that is, I was aware of the sensation, able to get up, able to get to the toilet and able to get most of the flow in the toilet rather than in the diaper. Somewhat frustrating, however, was that every time I sat up to get out of bed, that bending of the body caused there to be some immediate discharge of urine. By the fourth and fifth night, I was able to get up several times during the evening and as a result of that, have a significantly dry diaper in the morning as opposed to the first few days when there was no control at all.

One of the other aspects of this phase of the recovery is the concern with sitting. You will be advised to buy a doughnut to sit on–those big rubber half-innertube-looking things–and to only sit for 45 minutes or less at a time. Frankly, I found that the doughnut was painful rather than relieving, so maybe some better-cushioned seats will work for you as they did for me.

Every time I changed position from sitting to standing or standing to sitting, there was, by that musculature contraction, an almost uncontrolled - albeit very brief - leaking of urine. What I began to do with increasing success was to every so often just go to the bathroom and try to urinate in the toilet rather than in the diaper. It worked pretty well, although it was nowhere near 100%. I also found that I could sit longer on well-cushioned chairs and that, during that time, I had no leaking and stayed quite dry. Almost every time I stood up, there was that immediate sensation, so I tried the Kegel exercise until I could get to the toilet. This took practice, and I must confess it was somewhat frustrating and occasionally a little bit depressing.

At this point, it was really just a matter of time. I found myself able to be significantly alert mentally, certainly sufficiently to do some work, though by no means did I attempt to go to the office or be around other people. The incontinence, the periodic uncontrolled leaking, and the certain need for changing the diaper were just not something that I was interested in doing in an office full of wide-eyed and curious well-wishers and employees.

Conclusion

Among the many things that this whole process taught me are how frail we are and how there's absolutely no person who is immune to cancer. Throughout my life, I have been Mr. Lucky and Mr. Bulletproof. I've always been the guy that if there was trouble, and there was likely to be a fight or some kind of major problem, it was always, "Hit 'em, Cheney." Cheney was the guy who could get in there and go, and Cheney did so around the country and other parts of the world. Then I became a trial lawyer and for the last 50 years answered the bell to try every kind of horrible criminal case that you can imagine—kidnappings, murders, tortures, rapes, loots, pillaging; the winnable, the unwinnable; the popular, the unpopular; the outrageous; the sickening; the high profile; the unknown. Never having a fear of losing and very rarely doing so, I simply wasn't ready to think that cancer was going to get me. It had gotten my friends— several of them. Statistically, I should have had some protection by that, but the fact of the matter is, according to medical science, everybody's going to get prostate cancer if they live long enough—every man, that is—if he lives long enough and doesn't die from something else. What I hope for is that by being aware of our vulnerability, we can make the best out of every day of our lives, not take unnecessary chances and do what we can to try to prevent cancer. If you do receive the diagnosis that I did, then at least go into it with a positive attitude, knowing that you can be cured of it. Prostate cancer remains the second leading killer of men in the United States right after lung problems, but prostate cancer is also the singularly most treatable form of cancer if it is detected and treated early enough.

I believe that medical science, as it continues to develop, is bound to come up with ways to change the odds and the statistics and perhaps even have a method of absolute prevention, if not cure. The advances have been many over the last several years. The use of the DaVinci Robotic Surgery with laparoscopic procedure is remarkable compared to the traditional open surgery, which was the only method of removing a cancerous prostate for decades and decades.

I am absolute proof of its success. On the 13th day after I had the surgery, I walked two miles. On the 15th day I was back up to three miles a day. If I had had the open surgery, there would be no way in the world I would be able to do that. As a matter of fact, I would still be on a catheter for a month. So that is a very encouraging sign of development and advances. The awareness of dietary implications, the optimistic impact of lycopene, the optimistic impact of green tea, and other antioxidants are all things that portend good news for the future. Then, of course, with the recovery, we have all the drugs to assist with erectile function: Viagra or Cialis. All of these things tend to lessen the impact and help with recovery and maintaining a full life.

And, of course, that is the bottom line—life. I have it. I will continue to have it.

Glossary Of Supplies Needed Post-Surgery

1. A hospital bed. Most medical supply companies rent these, and some will require a doctor's order so they can submit the cost to insurance. This might be important depending on the daily or weekly charge they require.

2. Be sure to have an electrical outlet close to where you place the hospital bed for its operation.

3. From a medical supply company, obtain at least one cloth pad to put on the bed for leakage. Buy two packs of plastic pads that can be thrown away. These are very useful for use on the bed and also for placing on other furniture where the patient will sit.

4. Obtain a walker. It may not be necessary to use for walking, but it is very useful and handy in helping the patient get up and down. It also makes a great place to hang the catheter bag and particularly have it available once the patient tries to move around the room.

5. Be certain to have a prescription for anti-nausea medicine before leaving the hospital.
6. Gas-X. This should be prescribed to deal with bloating and constipation post-surgery.
7. A thermometer for checking temperatures in case of possible fevers.
8. Bandages and Neosporin. These may be needed in connection with the drainage tube hole.
9. Alcohol and cotton pads for cleaning the ends of the catheter and wiping down other things.
10. Medical adhesive tape. The cloth type worked best for taping the catheter tube onto the leg.
11. Depends. The "adjustable" ones are great for after the surgery. They have Velcro-like tabs, so you don't have to slip them over a foot. They are easier to use.
12. Bendable straws. Think about how difficult it is to drink when you are lying flat.
13. Supply of Gatorade or Pedialyte. A supply of popsicles is also a good item to have on hand. Not red.

14. When your patient comes out of the surgery recovery room, it is helpful to have some small chips of ice available so that he can have some moisture in the throat that is going to be sore from the anesthesia instrument.
15. Have available e-mail addresses for friends and family, all of whom will be interested in the patient's condition. They will be interested and acting in great concern, but the incessant and repeated numbers could be disturbing as a simple e-mail to everyone will handle providing the information.
16. Be sure that you have a couple of friends available who can run some errands, like picking up lunch or dinner for you.
17. A journal so that you can make daily entries of the medications taken, the amount of urine collection, the color of the urine samples, and also make comments that may or may not be of some importance at a later time.

About the Authors

J. Cheney Mason is a nationally renowned criminal defense lawyer having over 52 years of experience. He is board-certified by the National Board of Trial Advocacy and the Florida Bar Association, and a fellow of the American Board of Criminal Trial Lawyers. He is a former Director of the National Association of Criminal Defense Lawyers and also served as an NGO representative for the National Association of Criminal Defense Lawyers to the United Nations in Vienna, Austria. He is a former President of the Florida Association of Criminal Defense Lawyers. He has received the highest awards given annually by both the National Association of Criminal Defense Lawyers and the Florida Association of Criminal Defense Lawyers. In addition to numerous legal periodical articles, he has also published *Justice in America:: How Prosecutors and the Media Conspire against the Accused*. He is now retired from the active practice of criminal defense law but acts as a consultant and advisor to numerous lawyers and entities.

Jeffrey Richard Thill, M.D. is a Board Certified Urologist, having that certification for nearly 30 years. He is the surgeon who operated on Mr. Mason, and he currently works part-time at the Urology Institute of Central Florida. Dr. Thill performed the first robotic surgery at Florida Hospital in 2004. Dr. Thill's formal education included obtaining his B.A. (Summa Cum Laude) from McPherson College, McPherson, Kansas, M.D. degree from the University of Iowa, and completed his urology residency at the University of Florida in 1993, then served as a Clinical Professor of Urology at Shands Hospital at the University of Florida. From 1993 to 2007, he received a succession of awards for his excellence in understanding and teaching urology issues consistently for over 20 years, he maintains active participation in the Florida Urology Society and American Urology Association.

Made in the USA
Columbia, SC
07 January 2025